fundraising

Jenny Barlow

TEACH YOURSELF BOOKS

For UK order queries: please contact Bookpoint Ltd, 130 Milton Park, Abingdon, Oxon
OX14 4SB. Telephone: (44) 01235 827720. Fax: (44) 01235 400454. Lines are open from
9.00–18.00, Monday to Saturday, with a 24-hour message answering service.
Email address: orders@bookpoint.co.uk

A catalogue record for this title is available from The British Library.

ISBN 0 340 80393 2

First published 2002
Impression number   10 9 8 7 6 5 4 3 2 1
Year   2006 2005 2004 2003 2002

The 'Teach Yourself' name and logo are registered trade marks of Hodder & Stoughton Ltd.

Illustrations: Darin Mount

Typeset by Transet Limited, Coventry, England.
Printed in Great Britain for Hodder & Stoughton Educational, a division of Hodder
Headline Plc, 338 Euston Road, London NW1 3BH by Cox & Wyman Ltd, Reading,
Berkshire.

CONTENTS

FOREWORD

It seems a bit egotistical to be writing an introduction to a book on fundraising. That's not because we don't think we're capable of jotting down a few words on the subject (whether or not it makes for riveting reading is another matter) – it's more to do with the fact that even after a number of years of fundraising, we're still learning.

When Comic Relief began in 1985 there was no master plan – just the deeply felt conviction that something had to be done to try and help change things. Seventeen years and eight Red Nose Days down the line, this conviction is as strong as ever.

A good starting point for any aspiring fundraiser is the belief that every single person can make a difference, whoever they are and whatever they do. If you have the ability to instil this belief in your public, you're already at a huge advantage.

There are a few other key ingredients which will help to make your fundraising venture a success. At the risk of stating the ridiculously obvious, creativity is one of the most important. In an already over-crowded marketplace, if you can think up original and inspiring ways to catch people's attention and spark their enthusiasm, then you're well on your way.

Other useful assets will include flexibility (back up plans are essential), the ability to operate on fantastically tight budgets and of course, a sense of humour. Having fun is an integral part of the process.

But probably the most important ingredient – certainly for everyone involved with Comic Relief – is passion. That's what forms the foundation of all the work we do – and with that as your cornerstone, it really is astounding what you can achieve.

Michele Settle
Head of Fundraising, Comic Relief

For Christopher, Guy and Sam

INTRODUCTION

It's a great big, tough, old world out there. And these days it seems every other person is trying to squeeze a little compassion from everyone else in the effort to raise funds for a million genuinely good causes.

So many friends, neighbours and colleagues making house-to-house collections, standing outside Sainsbury's with a tin or writing to Tesco with urgent requests for funds. So many charities and institutions, from schools to churches and hostels to hospices, are in need of support. New ones are joining the fray every day. All this competition makes fundraising a pretty daunting task, especially if you are starting from scratch with little or no support from anyone else.

This book sets out to make that daunting task a little easier, to make sure that you are as well-prepared for the challenge ahead as you possibly can be. It will guide you through the mass of technical, legal and operational details that need to be considered before making your first approach for funding. What are the benefits of charitable status? How do you recruit volunteers, a patron or a managing committee? How should you prepare a 'case for support'? And how can you identify potential donors whether corporate, institutional or individual?

Which fundraising techniques will best suit your situation? Should you attempt to run a major fundraising event or would you be better off appealing to trusts, foundations or companies for funds? Are your skills and resources sufficient to manage a campaign through the press or would house-to-house and street collections be more appropriate? How can you promote your cause and make sure that your approaches to donors are well-received? There are many uncertainties that this book will help you to resolve so that you can produce and implement an effective fundraising plan.

One thing is certain – the most successful fundraisers are not necessarily professionals, but they are the people who go about their business most professionally. And one of the fundamentals of professionalism is to be well prepared. This book should help you to adopt a totally professional approach to the task ahead.

- **Chapter 1** looks at the demands on fundraisers today and examines why fundraising is such a competitive business.
- **Chapter 2** gets down to basics and suggests a set of principles which any fundraiser should apply to his or her work. It tackles the issue of an 'organizational culture' and an administrative structure, and how to make use of the new technologies. It also looks at charity law, the rules that govern fundraising and the benefits of charitable status.
- **Chapter 3** helps you to set targets and budgets, and find the necessary resources in terms of manpower.
- **Chapter 4** puts essential tools in place – a 'mission statement', a donations policy and a 'case for support'. It also looks at the benefits of undertaking a 'SWOT' analysis.
- **Chapter 5** explains how to package your project or cause into a 'marketable product'.
- **Chapter 6** shows you how to pave the way for your fundraising approaches. It examines the promotional and PR techniques at your disposal.
- **Chapter 7** explores the sources of funding that you might be able to tap and helps you to assess which will respond best to your approaches.
- **Chapter 8** looks at the different fundraising methods available to you and helps you to choose between them.
- **Chapter 9** outlines the skills that will help you implement your plans. It gives advice on writing proposals, making presentations, negotiating and building relationships, as well as guiding you to further sources of help and advice.

■ **Chapter 10** brings everything together so that you can produce your own fundraising strategy. It includes samples of the key documents you will need to produce – a promotional plan, a 'proposal' and the fundraising strategy itself.

1 | THE CHALLENGE FACING FUNDRAISERS TODAY

There is no doubt that it is more difficult to raise money today than ever before. There are greater demands for charitable funds on a local, national and international scale. New charities emerge every day in response to new crises and evolving needs. Events on the world stage, such as the humanitarian disasters caused by wars in Kosovo, Sudan and Sierra Leone, or catastrophes of nature such as earthquakes in India and flooding in Mozambique, demand a charitable response from all of us able to give. But there are also major changes in our own society that are placing an ever-increasing burden on the voluntary sector.

Successive governments have adopted more and more radical policies towards public spending as our expectations and demands for education, health and social services increase. The result has been a shift in the balance of funding from statutory to private and voluntary sources.

Many vulnerable members of our society have been transferred from institutions into **community care**. Whatever the benefits or otherwise to the individuals concerned and those who care for them, and whatever the advantages to government in terms of financial savings, the fact is that this policy increases the workload of voluntary organizations. Combined with the increasing age of our population this leads to an ever-growing demand for funds for community care.

Also, as a result of government policy, there are **changes in the health service** that are having a major impact on the fundraising scene. Where once the National Health Service might have been expected to serve all our health-care needs from major surgery to dentistry, changes in its structure in recent years have produced major changes in its funding. It is now commonplace to find health-care organizations competing for voluntary funding, and local support groups tapping every possible source of income for new and sophisticated equipment.

As **equipment for schools** becomes more sophisticated so does the need to produce an income from voluntary sources. The statutory funding which once provided for all the needs of the education system has failed to grow with our aspirations for our children's education. Most Parent Teacher Associations will consider fundraising a major part of their remit. Equally most schools will run fundraising activities to help support other causes.

Whether it is a good or a bad thing for the voluntary sector the impact of the **National Lottery** cannot be ignored. It may well be that the impulse of giving to charities by individuals has been adversely affected since the lottery began, but it is also true that a major new source of funding has emerged. The lottery certainly throws down a challenge to fundraisers.

And even outside the sphere of government there have been changes that affect fundraisers. Most notable of these is the entry of many **churches** onto the fundraising scene. Where years ago the Church of England owned vast tracts of land and financed many of our country's churches, there is now less funding from central sources. Individual churches have to pay for the cost of their own ministries as well as the maintenance of very old buildings, bringing many of them into the voluntary funding sector. Besides seeking money to support themselves the churches do, of course, have a mission to raise funds for other deserving causes.

A few facts about charities

'Money breeds money' so the saying goes – and this is just as true in the charity sector as anywhere else. The larger charities – those with an annual income of over £10 million – represent only 1 per cent of the total number of charities but they generate over 40 per cent of the sector's total income. While they will find it commonplace to pick up £1,000 here or there it will be a major achievement for a smaller organization.

- There are 187,000 registered charities in the UK.
- Over 90 per cent of charities have an annual income of less than £100,000.
- Over 90 per cent of charities account for only 6 per cent of the charitable sector income.

The response of fundraisers – and the implications for you

Fundraisers have risen to the challenges and responded to the ever-increasing demands for funds with more sophisticated techniques and growing professionalism. Which means, of course, that to compete successfully you must be as much, if not more, professional than the rest.

But while we strive to be businesslike we should not forget that fundraising can, and should, be fun! Fundraising is a 'people business' where who you know and how you relate to them can have an enormous impact on your achievements. The networking that is a part of successful fundraising will bring you into contact with all sorts of different people – some very talented, some highly skilled and others simply good to be with. The close working relationships that develop during a fundraising project can be enormously satisfying and lead to lasting friendships.

The challenges that fundraising offers can be highly motivating and extremely satisfying once met. There is nothing quite like the glow of success when, after months of effort, you are presented with the cheque that will enable your vital project.

Like many other things in life, one of the keys to success in fundraising is confidence. It can be pretty frightening tackling anything that is completely new. But confidence comes as knowledge and experience grow. This book will give you the knowledge to go out and gain the experience.

With the help of this guide you can be sure that you are tackling the fundraising task professionally and thoroughly. Each of the following chapters will guide you logically through the preparatory steps that every dedicated and successful fundraiser will make as

Knowing that you have made a difference makes it all worthwhile.

he or she starts to fundraise. The book culminates in the creation of the fundraising plan – a clear and appropriate strategy that you will be able to implement in total confidence. All you need to do then is to go out and enjoy it!

Questions and answers

How can I compete?

Q *So many people are trying to raise funds from the same donors. How can I compete with the big charities and their exciting projects?*

A Don't be put off! On the whole the big charities will be tapping different sources for their income – many will be working on a national scale while you will be concentrating on local donors.

But even if you do compete head on, perhaps with the local branch of a national charity, remember that the donor might be more motivated by your cause or project. It helps to present your case effectively, but most important is finding the right person to give to you. Read on! This book was written to teach you the tricks of the trade and to help you become just as professional as the professionals in the way you tackle fundraising.

Do I really need to put in so much effort?

Q *I've just been asked to help raise money for the school PTA. Surely I don't have to bother about being 'professional'. Isn't it just a case of rattling a tin and running a cake stall at the school fete?*

A Fundraising can take as much or as little effort as you wish – but the more you put in the more you will achieve. The principles of fundraising that you will find in this book can be applied to any fundraising task, however small. You may find yourself inspired to do more than rattle the tin and bake a few cakes!

2 | CULTURAL, LEGAL AND ADMINISTRATIVE FRAMEWORK

Knowing where to start is often the most daunting prospect of all. If all you have is a worthy cause, your own commitment to work for it and a desperate need for funds to support it, you might be forgiven for wondering how to begin. Putting some basic principles and ground rules into place will help to create a structure from within which you can make a disciplined and effective approach to fundraising.

Creating an appropriate working environment

You might call this simply 'standards of behaviour' and in many cases it will emerge naturally. Your culture is, essentially, the set of principles which everyone in your organization applies to their work – your way of going about things. If you work with others it is worth giving some time at the outset to agreeing a set of principles which will govern your behaviour. If you are the one and only representative of your charity or cause it will be easier to decide on these principles and to uphold them!

- Top of your list should be **professionalism**. There are too many good causes competing for too little money. Unless you are entirely businesslike (especially in your dealings with businesses) you will not be one of the winners.
- Fundraising is all about 'selling' an idea, and it can be very tempting to elaborate on the idea when trying to convince someone to 'buy'. But never be tempted to offer more than you can deliver. The **honesty and integrity** with which you approach your donors and

> the long-term trust that you build with them is far more important than any short-term gain.

- There are many different techniques that you can apply to your fundraising. Whichever you choose, much of what you achieve will be down to hard graft and **persistence**. Under the same heading you could add **commitment**. Donors respond to genuine dedication.

- With so many competing causes it is imperative to **seize opportunities** as they come. Your organization should pride itself on being alert to what is going on outside so that you can link in your own activities.

- Fundraising is all about people – asking and receiving, giving and taking. Establishing a culture that uses **personal contact** wherever possible will be immensely beneficial. No amount of circulars or mail shots will achieve the results that a phone call or meeting can.

This list of principles has been tried and tested over many years, but it evolved originally from Sam Clarke's list in the excellent *The Complete Fundraising Handbook,* published by the Directory of Social Change (see the Appendix for DSC's address).

Making the ask

The aspect of fundraising that causes more discomfort than any other is that of 'making the ask' – actually asking someone for money. There are two issues here. Firstly a resistance in some organizations to asking for money from certain sources, and secondly a cultural reluctance to approach others for money.

Most fundraisers come to terms with the necessity of asking for money from any appropriate source pretty quickly, but others in the organization might not be so relaxed about it. Many charities suffer from conflicts between project-based staff and fundraising staff over the issue of funding and where it comes from.

As it is fundamental to what we are talking about here, and to the business of most charities, it is essential that you address any concerns about asking others for money if you come across resistance in your own organization. Usually explaining the need for funds will help to persuade other colleagues that asking for money is a necessary evil. Involving all staff and volunteers in the development of a fundraising or donations policy that defines any 'no go areas' can help to convince them that their principles need not be compromised. Chapter 4 looks at this in more detail.

The hard fact is that fundraising is about 'selling' your organization to potential donors. You and your colleagues need to be comfortable with this idea. Good communication internally, listening to concerns and explaining needs, will go a long way to resolving any differences.

Case study

A major, national charity had a high staff turnover and poor morale. One of the key issues that had led to this unhappiness was tension between project departments and fundraising departments over sources of income. The project teams accused the fundraisers of 'making the tail wag the dog' – of fundraising for the sake of it from any source and trying to create new projects on which to spend the money raised. The fundraisers accused the project teams of being inflexible and unhelpful, and of ignoring the harsh realities of generating income.

Finally the chief executive organized an away day for all those involved to discuss their concerns. The session was designed to be relaxed and informal but was carefully chaired to ensure fair play. As each side started to understand the other's point of view a concensus began to emerge about more acceptable fundraising practice and more supportive behaviour from the project teams.

After the event, and based on its conclusions, a 'code of practice' was drawn up which every member of the fundraising and project teams signed. It takes time for cultures to change but this was the starting point for greatly improved cooperation and communication, which, in its turn, improved staff morale and turnover.

If the problem you face is your own reluctance to ask for money, you will find that focusing on your cause and its needs will provide motivation. Many fundraising mechanisms offer donors something in return so make yourself focus on the benefits they will receive through the process of giving. And remember that practice makes perfect. The more often you ask for money, the easier it becomes. The very thorough preparation that this book will help you to put in place will give you the confidence you need for your first attempts.

Confidence breeds success, and it can be highly motivating for the entire organization if you are prepared to share your successes with your colleagues. Sharing the highs – and lows – with other staff and volunteers will help build a close-knit and more effective team. In any context people work better together when they are enjoying themselves. In the world of fundraising, think how an event can sparkle if all those involved can't think of anything they would rather be doing!

Celebrating success will motivate everyone.

Charity law

On a more serious note, obviously you will wish to operate within the bounds of the law – and ignorance offers no protection. You must make it your business to acquaint yourself with any relevant legislation which may apply whether you are a registered charity or not. It is beyond the scope of this book to go into detail about all aspects of the law and Charity Commission guidance relating to fundraising. Instead the following paragraphs summarize the key points and tell you where to find further advice.

The requirements for all fundraisers in England and Wales (whether working for registered or non-registered organizations) are contained in the Charities Act 1993 and further advice on its implications can be sought from the Charity Commission for England and Wales. (Helpline telephone number and address are in the Appendix.) Charities and fundraising in Scotland are regulated principally by the Law Reform (Miscellaneous Provisions) (Scotland) Act 1990 and those in Northern Ireland by The Charities Act (Northern Ireland) 1964. Advice on legal issues is offered by the Department of Health and Social Services Voluntary Activity Unit – Charities Branch in Northern Ireland and Scottish Charities Office in Scotland – addresses and phone numbers in the Appendix.

Applying for charitable status in England and Wales

A charity is defined as an organization set up to provide something of benefit to others in society. It must have purposes which are exclusively charitable. There is no general statutory definition of 'charitable purposes' but the broad headings currently used by the Charity Commission are:

■ the relief of financial hardship
■ the advancement of education
■ the advancement of religion
■ other charitable purposes for the benefit of the community.

The Register of Charities in England and Wales was first set up 35 years ago but the common understanding of what is 'charitable' has continued to evolve. Consequently the Charity Commission is undertaking a Review of the Register and may amend the boundaries of charitable status.

Legally charities as defined above must normally register with the Charity Commission if any of the following applies:

- the organization has a total income of more than £1,000 a year
- the organization owns or occupies land with or without buildings
- the organization has permanent endowment.

An organization that does not meet these criteria is referred to as an 'excepted charity' and is not required to register but may ask to be registered on a voluntary basis. It will then be subject to the charity jurisdiction of the High Court. Check with the Charity Commission to see if you need to register – there are exceptions. Sports clubs set up to benefit members, town twinning associations and organizations set up to promote political views are among those not eligible for charitable status. If your organization is set up solely to raise funds – perhaps for another charity – and your trustees have no discretion as to how the funds are used, you will not be able to register as a charity.

Benefits and drawbacks of charitable status

So what does charitable status mean for fundraisers? Firstly it may be a legal requirement that your charity is registered (see above), and secondly there are benefits and responsibilities attached to registration. The main advantages of charitable status involve tax exemptions. But the reassurance that your charity is bona fide may influence the decision-making process of donors, from members of the public through to local government. Some funders insist on charitable status for their recipients, particularly for start-up funding.

On the down side, being a registered charity may limit your activities, particularly, from a fundraiser's point of view, the opportunity to trade.

Charity Commission Publications

Fortunately the Charity Commission produces a series of free publications which offer further guidance on the law in relation to charities. Guidance on what charities can and cannot do as far as trading is concerned can be found in the Charity Commission publication CC35 'Charities and Trading'. For further advice on the legal implications of fundraising request CC20 'Charities and Fundraising' and for advice on registration ask for CC21 'Starting and Registering a Charity'. Other leaflets offer guidance on accounting, the responsibilities of trustees, political activities and campaigning, investments and insurance. All of these publications and many others are available on the Internet or can be ordered through the Charity Commission Publications Office – address, phone number and website in the Appendix.

Professional fundraisers

If you choose to employ a fundraising consultant or agency, or if you enter into a joint promotion with a company, there are further regulations in force covered in CC20 'Charities and Fundraising'. Essentially there must be a written agreement between the parties, and any funds acquired by the professional fundraiser or commercial participator must be paid to the charity without any fees or expenses deducted. These are, of course, sensible measures designed for the protection of charities.

Charities in Scotland and Northern Ireland

Charities in Scotland and Northern Ireland are recognized by the Inland Revenue which maintains a public index and gives each charity a reference number. The Scottish Charities Office and the Voluntary Activity Unit – Charities Branch in Belfast – offer telephone enquiry lines and publish further helpful information. Telephone numbers and addresses can be found in the Appendix.

Tax issues

The issues surrounding fundraising and tax continue to evolve and it is advisable to seek advice from either the Inland Revenue or Customs and Excise (contact details in the Appendix) on any question of tax liability. Do bear in mind that some fundraising events may be subject to tax, although a one-off event that is run exclusively to raise funds for a charity, such as a ball, dance, fete, fair, car boot sale, jumble sale, auction, raffle or lottery will probably be tax exempt.

Putting systems and facilities in place

Around your project or cause you need to build a structure that will support your fundraising efforts. If you are a trustee of your charity you will be legally responsible for the general control and management of your organization. A full explanation of the role and responsibilities of a trustee is published by the Charity Commission in its leaflet CC3 'Responsibilities of Charity Trustees'. But whatever your status within the organization it is imperative for all concerned that your systems are watertight.

If you are to bring money in you must make sure that you have sound financial systems and controls in place. It doesn't matter how simple these are provided that all incoming funds go immediately into a separate account set up for this purpose and that you log effectively all incoming and outgoing funds. You should be aware of your financial situation on a daily basis – working to a budget that predicts income and expenditure is essential – and you must be able to produce a balance sheet at the end of each year. You may wish to employ the services of an accountant or appoint a treasurer to handle such matters as your books should be audited by an independent financial authority annually. If you are a charity with income or expenditure of over £10,000 you have a statutory obligation to submit accounts to the Charity Commission.

It is sensible to have more than one person present when money is counted or paid in to the bank, and you should have more than one signatory for issuing cheques. Get to know your bank manager if you can!

The key points to remember are:

- Prepare and work to a budget.
- Log all incoming and outgoing funds.
- Produce an annual budget sheet.
- Pay all incoming funds into one account set up solely for the purpose.
- Have two signatures on cheques.

Wherever you have your office, you need to be organized.

Whether you are paid or unpaid, working from an office or from the kitchen table, you need to organize the paperwork to back up your fundraising. You will need administrative systems even if they are operated just by you and your word processor. This phase of setting up can be very satisfying as your ideas begin to take tangible form. This is the base from which your fundraising can take off!

The key tasks are:

- dealing with written correspondence
- dealing with telephone enquiries/personal callers

■ filing
■ constantly updating your database of contacts
■ disseminating information.

It is easy to be thrilled by an incoming donation but forget to say thankyou. Your systems should ensure that every gift is acknowledged and that the name of the benefactor is recorded on your database for future use. Anyone who tries to contact you should be welcomed, even if it is by an answerphone that promises – and you deliver – an early response.

Every person who shows an interest in your organization is a 'prospect' for fundraising purposes and you must make the most of each one. Start a file or database of all potential supporters and update it regularly. If you can afford to invest there are a number of 'contact management packages' to help you do this. The Raiser's Edge is one of the most tried and tested fundraising database packages, but there are many others available. Talk to other voluntary groups to find out what they use and would recommend.

Don't forget to tell the world outside – and others inside your organization – about your activities. If you mail a regular newsletter you won't forget to pass on vital information. And although filing is the bugbear of many a fundraiser's life, having a system for it will, at least, mean that you can find that vital document when you need it!

Most of all you must be able to communicate with other people – volunteers, supporters and potential donors – verbally and in writing. Access to a telephone, a fax machine and a word processor for producing professional letters, proposals and other documents is just about essential. If you don't have these your most immediate task will be to try to borrow, share or rent (at a concessional rate) office space and facilities. Other small voluntary organizations might be prepared to share their space and equipment. Sometimes companies will loan a desk in their own offices as part of their charitable effort. Or contact Gifts in Kind UK which acts as a giant clearing house for businesses to donate surplus goods and equipment to the voluntary sector (contact details in the Appendix).

Applying for start-up funds

Many donors will consider providing start-up funds and you may be lucky enough to secure such funding from trusts, individuals, companies or even statutory sources. But the process can be slow and you may find that you have made a considerable outlay from your own pocket before any outside grants materialize. You would be wise to research the opportunities available to you locally and follow the advice offered throughout this book before making any approaches – including those for start-up funds.

Working with the new technologies

As in any other office, a computer with access to the Internet and the capacity to send and receive electronic mail is almost always an asset. If you are comfortable with the new technologies, are disciplined in the way you use them, and can afford them, they can greatly enhance your fundraising efforts. However, it is very easy to be distracted by umpteen incoming e-mails or to lose yourself in the depths of the 'web'. Beware the pitfalls, but used wisely the Internet is a powerful research tool and e-mails have revolutionized communications.

Besides researching on the Internet and communicating by e-mail you may wish to set up a website for your organization. Make sure that this would be cost-effective and that your targeted supporters would find it. Young people regard the Internet as an unremarkable way to gather information. Millions have acquired the habit of communicating 'online'. Other people may not have access to the Internet or even have heard of the term 'website'.

The cost of developing a website need not be excessive and no advanced technical knowledge is needed to create a few simple but eye-catching pages. You could flag up your mission statement, illustrate achievements and successes, and promote ongoing appeals. As a website is a promotional tool read Chapter 6 to check for alternatives and to put websites into a broader context.

Don't be afraid of the new technologies. If you think your organization could benefit from using them but you don't know much about them, enrol on one of the many courses that are available through local authorities to teach you the basics. Or ask a computer literate friend to spend some time teaching you.

Some of the key benefits to fundraisers include:

- The projection of a more professional image to potential donors, especially those in the corporate sector who take the new technologies for granted and who might be surprised if they can't e-mail you.
- Swifter and more versatile communication with other Internet users – being able, for example, to send documents for amendment or approval instantly.
- Enormous pools of research material at your fingertips. If you have access to the Internet, you should never make an approach to a company without delving into its website first.
- Dissemination of information about your own organization if you can afford to set up a website of your own.

Opportunities for research can be found in surprising places.

If you don't have access in your own office, there are plenty of libraries, cafés, and even railway stations and airports, where you can log in for short periods of research. Better still, ask a friend or a supportive company to allow you access from time to time.

Questions and answers

Working with others who oversell the project

Q *The director of our charity is always overselling our project to potential donors. I am the one who has to try to live up to his big ideas. How can I be principled and honest with our donors in this situation?*

A This is a tricky, but not uncommon, problem. Many directors, chief executives and trustees are quite remote from the sharp end of project management and fundraising. Usually the key to defusing the situation is good communication. Try a frank and open discussion of your difficulties with your director. Involve him in your activities and try to show him the situation from your perspective. If he understands the problems that you have in implementing his ideas you might be well on the way to solving those problems!

If the difficulty persists even when your director is fully aware of your concerns, you face a more serious problem. You might try enlisting the support and influence of a sympathetic trustee or senior staff member who can argue your case for you. Overselling can only be damaging to your charity and others may also wish to limit the damage. Working with other members of staff or trustees to bring about a more realistic approach may be the answer.

You must find a way to persuade your director that no donor wants to be promised one thing and given another. It may take time to bring about this change. Meanwhile you must try to walk the tightrope of remaining loyal to your director while being honest with your donors. Ultimately you must be true to yourself and should not compromise your own integrity. You must earn trust and respect from your donors – hopefully your director will too.

Overcoming nerves

Q *I want to help fundraise for our local hospice – a friend of mine has a child there – but I hate asking for money. How can I tackle this?*

A You could, of course, offer to help in some other way – maybe giving administrative support in the office or distributing promotional materials.

If you really do want to fundraise think of your friend's child first. Think how much that child needs the support that the hospice gives and how badly the hospice needs funds. It's much easier to ask when the need is so clear and so great. Donors will respect and be inspired by your commitment. Use this book to prepare thoroughly, and remember that the first time you ask will be the worst. As you become more confident it really will get easier and easier.

Applying for charitable status

Q *The whole question of charitable status worries me. I think my organization should apply but I'm almost afraid to ask in case we should have done it already.*

A The important thing is to get your house in order now. The Charity Commission is there to guide you and can give advice on whether you should apply for charitable status and if so how to go about it. It will help you through the process of registration and advise you how to produce a governing document for your charity. The Charity Commission publications are extremely helpful so send off for the ones that are relevant to you now (address in the Appendix). If you need further advice call the Charity Commission on the number in the Appendix.

I'm not used to working alone

Q *I've joined a small charity where I will be the only fundraiser, but I'm used to a busy office with a team of other people. What is the best way to cope with the isolation?*

A Don't worry. Fundraising is all about people. If you are to be successful as a fundraiser you will need to be out and about meeting people, not sitting in an office on your own. Try networking with others in a similar position to get you started. Go to conferences and exhibitions that are relevant to your work and talk to the people you meet there. Most of all make appointments to meet potential donors. Once you have really got going you will be glad of a quiet hour or two at the office!

3 | GEARING UP

Once the basic cultural, legal and administrative details have been taken care of you can start to think about the specific fundraising task ahead and what you need to do to complete it. Assessing the scale of the task and setting appropriate fundraising targets and budgets are crucial at this stage. You also need to decide whether you can handle the work on your own. If not, who should you recruit to help you and how do you find them?

Assessing the task

Have you stopped to think about your fundraising needs, the scale of the fundraising task facing you, how long it will take, and all that you will need to do to complete it? If not, take stock now – you will only be able to plan successfully if you know exactly what you are trying to achieve and how much time you have to get there. Start with the end in view.

Now might be a good time to have a 'brainstorming' session with other staff and volunteers, or, if you are working on your own, ask a friend who is sympathetic to your cause and understands what you are trying to achieve to brainstorm with you. The purpose of brainstorming is to generate as many ideas as you can that are relevant to the task ahead – in this case assessing your needs. New perspectives contributed by others will add enormously to your own outlook. The rules of brainstorming say that no idea should be dismissed and all ideas should be recorded. It will probably be up to you to make sense of many disparate thoughts afterwards, but you will find that a train of good ideas has emerged. Brainstorming sessions should be kept short to concentrate everyone's energies and to avoid the process becoming stale.

It is surprising how much more can be achieved by a group of people working together than by one person sitting alone.

Once your brainstorming is over and you have plenty of ideas about the task ahead, you might find it helpful to make a list, under separate headings, of all the costs that need to be met by your fundraising efforts, for example:

- **Project costs** – these may include building costs, running costs, staff costs etc.
- **Administrative costs** – the costs of all phoning, faxing, paperwork etc. that will be part of your fundraising effort as well as all the admin that is necessary to run the project itself.
- **Promotional costs** – to publicize your project and your fundraising efforts, for example leaflets, posters and advertisements.
- **Professional advice** – is the project so complex that you will need input from architects, surveyors, solicitors or other professionals? Unless they are giving their time free of charge you will have to raise funds to pay their substantial fees.

Likewise, you may find it helpful at this stage to produce a schedule of what you expect to happen when – allowing extra time for all that is beyond your own control! You could, also, conduct a simple feasibility study to assess whether your fundraising task is realistic. This might include looking at the success or otherwise of similar appeals in your area and sounding out key people who you might wish to involve as committee members, volunteers or donors. Consider too where funds might come from. If you have never done any fundraising before it might be worth bearing in mind the model referred to as the 'pyramid of giving'. This demonstrates that most fundraising campaigns will take a pyramid structure with one or two large donations at the top but the base of support coming from a mass of small ones. How will you generate these?

Obviously there is a limit to how far all this speculation can go and some questions will only be answered as you start to fundraise, but it is wise to have done your homework.

Setting targets

Setting a target will be easier in some cases than in others. If, for example, you have taken on responsibility for raising the funds to buy a kidney dialysis machine, or a set of play equipment for your local nursery school, or a new organ for the church, you have a self-contained 'project'. This means that your goal is finite and you can set a target that is quantifiable.

Much more difficult is the prospect of setting targets where funds are needed to cover the ongoing running costs (usually known as core costs) of an existing charity or project. These might include anything and everything from salaries and rents right through to paper clips and envelopes. If there is no obvious end to the funding need, you must create one for the purpose of your own strategic planning, even if it is only defined by a year or period end. So, you can set a target to raise x by the end of this year and y in the whole of next.

It is far better though, to divide your funding need into individual projects, each with its own separate fundraising target, which should include running costs. We will look at packaging and presenting those projects for funding later in the book. Meanwhile, suffice to say, it will be much easier to meet the targets for neat, self-contained projects than for an amorphous cost-covering exercise. However you choose to define your targets there are two golden rules that apply:

- Every fundraising exercise should have a target that is **measurable**. Both your own motivation and the support of others will depend on the fact that you have a clear and precise target and that you know how far you have gone towards reaching it.
- All targets should be **realistic** and **achievable**. Far too many fundraisers struggle to achieve targets, either self-imposed or created by others, that are totally unrealistic. It may be difficult to confront this situation and to remedy it, especially if your fund-raising target has been set by someone further up the organizational hierarchy than yourself. But it is quite pointless to work towards an unachievable goal. Ultimately this can only be damaging for yourself and for your organization. Make it your business, therefore, to ensure that your fundraising target is commensurate with your skills and resources.

Setting budgets

Relative to your fundraising target will be your fundraising budget. You will have to spend money to raise money – you will need to produce promotional materials, to travel to meet potential donors and to communicate with them by phone, fax, letter or e-mail. You may have to pay a fundraiser, either as a member of staff or as a consultant. This is sensible, logical and standard practice, and there is no reason why you should feel guilty about it. But the word 'relative' is important.

Most charities aim to achieve a minimum cost/income ratio of 1:5 over a range of activities and a period of time, but it is better practice to try for 1:10. This means that £1 is spent for every £10 raised. In the early stages of a fundraising drive the ratio might be much lower – you may need to invest to build a database for example, or to launch a corporate fundraising campaign that may take some time to produce results. Some fundraising exercises will be more profitable than others. If you can raise money without incurring any costs, all well and good. But if you cannot, do allow yourself a tightly controlled cost-covering or expenses budget in order to achieve your fundraising targets.

Key budget headings might be:

- **Confirmed income** – e.g. grants, covenants, sponsorship and royalty payments.
- **Predicted income** – e.g. profits from planned events, raffle income, donations.
- **Expenditure** – e.g. office costs, staff costs, leaflet production, presentation costs, travel costs.

Whatever applies to your own personal situation, make sure that your accounts balance and that you can afford to spend when you are likely to incur costs. Cash flow management is an art to which not all mere mortals can aspire – but do prepare your budget with dates of in-comings and out-goings as precisely as possible to avoid financial embarrassment.

Recruiting and retaining staff and volunteers

You may be in the unenviable position of facing a major fundraising task alone and without any outside help. Or are you? Even if your project or cause is very much self-motivated and driven, you may be able to recruit others to support you – if that is what you wish. Now is the time to decide whether you go it alone or whether you recruit others – paid staff or volunteers, individuals or a committee – to help reach your fundraising goal.

As with any other task you are more likely to be successful in recruiting both staff and volunteers if you **plan** carefully first. You should take time to assess why you need help and when. You should consider how many people you need, but equally whether you have the resources, such as office space and equipment to use these extra hands effectively.

Producing a **staff or volunteer profile** will help you to identify the sort of person you need. Consider the skills and experience that the task demands and that will complement your own. Take a close look at the personality of potential partners. If you are likely to find a particular person difficult to work with it may be better to recruit someone else.

Make sure that you have a **job description** for staff members and a **description of duties** for volunteers that has clear objectives for each individual and a reporting structure. While the help of volunteers may be critical to your success and is given, usually, out of goodwill, it is essential that the best interests of your organization are served by all who work for it.

Case study

Tony Dogood was delighted to have found a useful role as a volunteer for a local charity in his retirement. He met one of the trustees, who happened to be a good friend of his, to discuss his new role over a pint in the pub. The trustee told him about the dire need for funds and commented that the charity might try its hand at corporate fundraising. Within a few days Tony had contacted the PR manager from his old company and had secured a donation of £500. Unfortunately this soured the pitch of the charity's paid fundraiser who had just submitted a proposal to the managing director of the same company for £5,000 worth of support!

The secret of **finding staff and volunteers** is to go out and look for them! While some good people may come to you of their own volition, many others will not even consider giving their time and expertise unless they are asked. Spread the word through all your contacts; approach your local Voluntary Service Bureau (VSB) which will have a register of volunteers and REACH (Retired Executives Action Clearing House – see the Appendix) which keeps lists of people with business or professional skills who would be willing to help in exchange for reasonable expenses; try local organizations such as Women's Institutes, Townswomen's Guilds,

Rotary and Round Table groups; and advertise if need be through the local press or in shop windows and at the library. For paid staff advertise in relevant charity and business magazines.

Do feel that you can **interview** potential volunteers as well as potential paid staff. It has to be in their interests as much as yours to make sure that you are compatible and that the volunteer can handle the task. If you decide you want this particular person on your team make sure you discuss the benefits of joining your group as well as being open about any difficulties.

Taking the trouble to welcome a new staff member or volunteer is the first step towards **retaining** a good person. Maintaining regular contact, training where necessary, keeping your team focused on its task and thanking them are also essential.

Forming a fundraising committee

It may not be your style to manage by committee but it is one way of spreading the workload. Some of your volunteers may have particularly relevant skills and experience, or they may have a wealth of contacts. These could be put to good use through the committee structure. You may be in the situation where a committee exists already – in which case you must manage it effectively.

On the benefit side, committees offer opportunities for:

- sharing the workload and responsibilities
- sharing and generating ideas and enthusiasm
- motivating key volunteers by giving them an important role
- tapping the skills of those (especially business people) who might not volunteer in any other way
- networking and generating contacts
- giving credibility to your cause and your methods.

Disadvantages of committees can be:

- potential infighting and 'power politics'
- more cumbersome decision-making
- efforts less focused.

Roles and recruitment

The key roles in the fundraising committee are those of chairperson, secretary and treasurer. As with all other forms of recruitment, the key to success is to be proactive. Don't wait for someone to volunteer – go out and choose the best candidate. Use all your contacts to search for potential committee members and advertise if necessary.

Take care to recruit a **chairperson** who will have sufficient time for the task and whose strength of personality will not prevent him or her from working effectively as part of a team. Obviously someone with charisma and contacts who is willing and able to influence others will be an asset, as will someone who can chair a meeting efficiently.

If you intend to chair the committee yourself, be sure that you can do so efficiently.

If you can find someone who will organize meetings and take and circulate minutes efficiently – the role of **secretary** – you will free yourself of an administrative burden leaving more time for fundraising. Likewise, a **treasurer** who can manage the committee's accounts and expenses will liberate you.

Finding a patron

Although no more a necessity than the fundraising committee, it can be helpful to have a patron – someone of stature who can act as a figurehead for your cause. It is easier to make an approach through a personal contact than a cold letter and someone who has good reason to support you is, of course, more likely to accept the role. So look for celebrities, captains of industry or politicians who live locally and who might have an interest in your work. Then find someone who knows that person to approach them on your behalf.

Case study

Little Snoring's Church Organ Appeal wished to approach local rock star, Eric Collins, to be its – somewhat unlikely – patron. But for good reason, as Eric had been married in the church twenty years before. Fortunately, Mrs Char, secretary of the appeal, was also Eric's cleaner, and he accepted her invitation to be patron with pleasure!

Using agencies and consultants

There are many professional agencies that you might call on for strategic fundraising advice or to supplement your manpower – if you can afford it. The range of skills on offer is vast – everything from strategic planning to market research and PR. You can choose between large, commercially run agencies and single consultants who might operate part-time, often, in the charity world, while raising a family. Personal recommendations are usually the best way to find good external advice. The Institute of Charity Fundraising Managers (ICFM) and the National Council for Voluntary Organisations (NCVO) keep lists of freelance fundraisers and consultants (addresses and phone numbers in the Appendix).

Agencies and consultants do not generally come cheap (though fees differ enormously) but if you choose the right one you might find it cost-effective. Do select carefully. Discuss your needs with a number of different consultants rather than accepting a pitch from someone who targets you! Do make sure that you give the same clear brief to each. Don't expect free and detailed proposals, but do expect to be told what you will get for your money and what the consultancy should achieve.

Understandably there is a growing tendency to remunerate on a commission basis. But the Charity Commission and the ICFM code of practice advise against this as the system is open to malpractice. Paying for time given is recommended, but in this case it is all the more important that you choose the right adviser in the first place. According to the law there must be a written agreement between your charity and any professional fundraiser.

The ICFM can offer further advice on choosing and drawing up a contract with fundraising consultants – the address and phone number are in the Appendix.

Questions and answers

Being 'cost-effective'

Q *I help out a local charity which holds a ball annually as its major fundraiser. I've noticed that it raises a reasonable sum doing this, but that it spends almost as much to mount the event. What should the charity do?*

A This is a classic 'targets versus costs and budgets' question. The trustees and managers of the charity should take a hard look at the cost/income ratio of the event to decide whether this really is an effective fundraiser, whether there are ways of increasing the profit from the event, or whether other fundraising methods might be more appropriate.

If the event isn't already sponsored this could be a good way of improving cost-effectiveness. If a company or other benefactor covers the cost of holding the event, the proceeds will be pure profit. There may be ways of cutting costs or increasing prices and these should be explored too. But ultimately it is quite pointless to keep running an event that isn't more than paying its way. The time and resources that are sunk annually into the ball might be much better deployed running a street collection or a series of less ambitious and less expensive events.

Difficulty working with volunteers

Q *I have just joined a charity that has a small but dedicated group of volunteers who help with administration and fundraising. Unfortunately several of them are very 'stuck in their ways'. As the new paid fundraiser I would like to try some new methods of raising money but I am meeting resistance from the volunteers. How should I handle this?*

A   Firstly take heart – you are not alone. Managing change is a common problem, and one that is particularly acute in the voluntary sector where change is often necessary and vehemently opposed.

The first thing to recognize is that you are being paid by the charity to raise funds and you must do so to the best of your ability. So put aside your scruples. While you must be sensitive you must also bring about the change that is necessary.

If you wish to keep your volunteers you must win them over to the merits of your ideas. Start with communication. Have a frank exchange of views with your volunteers. Listen to their concerns and explain your point of view. You may each learn something from the other. Try a brainstorming session to spark creative ideas about fundraising. If your volunteers come up with new ideas of their own they may be less opposed to yours.

As you work on your fundraising strategy try to incorporate some of your volunteers' best ideas. These people do have a stake in the organization and may have some valuable knowledge and experience. The more they contribute to the fundraising plan the greater their ownership of it, and commitment to it, will be. Circulate a draft of the plan for their comments.

When the plan is complete present it to the volunteers with a rationale for every part of it. Explain why it may be necessary to try new methods and also how your volunteers can be part of the new regime. It may be that some resistance is built simply on fear of the unknown, so offer training in new techniques even if you can only afford to do it yourself in house. Explain the benefits that these new practices might bring to your volunteers in terms of job satisfaction, work load and opportunities for personal development. Explain too the benefits that new methods of fundraising may bring to your organization and its fundraising potential.

You may need to try some team building exercises to break down barriers and build trust. These can be as simple as a weekly lunch together at the pub or as dramatic as tackling an outdoor assault course. Use whichever seems appropriate!

If you do lose a volunteer or two look forward to recruiting someone who is absolutely right for the task. Don't be afraid to interview new recruits to your team even if they are unpaid. It is only fair to both parties that a clear set of duties is drawn up and that all expectations are understood. If you recruit carefully you should be able to build an excellent support team.

Working with agencies and consultants

Q *A friend in another charity suggested to me that I might ask several fundraising agents or consultants to pitch for the management of our new campaign. She said that we would pick up plenty of good ideas for running the campaign ourselves if we decided not to employ anyone. Is this ethical?*

A No, it certainly isn't, and if those of us who work in the charity sector cannot be honest with one another, who can?

It would be pretty underhand to ask one or more agencies and consultants to pitch for business with you if you have no intention of giving the work to any of them. While we should strive to be as professional as possible in all our dealings, there is no need for the charity world to pick up the worst of commercial habits!

An agency or consultancy will go to considerable time and effort to win new business. We should look to develop good working partnerships with the ones we choose to employ, and be honest in our dealings with the rest.

Fundraising for salaries

Q *Is it possible, and is it ethical, to seek sponsorship for salaries? I feel we should be able to pay our staff from our core income.*

A There's no reason why you shouldn't. In fact sponsoring a staff post can be quite a neat project to offer a corporate supporter.

The important thing is that the contract and agreed terms of your employee are in line with the funding that is available. So if a company is prepared to sponsor a staff post for two years, the post should only be offered on a two-year fixed-term contract. You may be able to offer the possibility of renewing the contract at the end of the term if you believe that your sponsor will renew or that some other funding source may be found.

Fewer and fewer jobs are 'for life' these days, both in the voluntary and commercial sectors. More workers expect to find fixed-term contracts and some prefer to work that way. The important thing is to treat your staff well while they are with you.

4 PREPARING ESSENTIAL TOOLS FOR FUNDRAISING

There are several tasks to be undertaken at this point that are absolutely fundamental to your success as a fundraiser. Before you go out and ask anyone for money it is essential that you and everyone else in your organization are clear and agreed about what you are trying to achieve and why – you need a 'mission statement'. You should also know whether you can accept donations from anyone, or whether there are any 'no go' areas – you should have a donations policy. And if you are to influence others to give, you need an effective 'case for support'. One of the most common causes of muddled and ineffective fundraising campaigns is a lack of preparation at this stage.

Preparing a mission statement

Successful fundraisers know precisely what their organization is – and what it is trying to achieve – in exactly the same way as a salesman knows the product he is trying to sell. Surprisingly, perhaps, not all organizations seeking funds are quite so clear about their purpose. If there is any doubt within your own organization, now is the time to thrash out a 'mission statement' and make sure that it is used by everyone.

Although it may sound like just another piece of worthless jargon, a mission statement, or 'vision' as it is sometimes known, is actually a very valuable tool. Likewise, the exercise of creating one is useful for any organization – charitable or otherwise. A mission statement is a succinct encapsulation of what your organization is or aspires to be, and what it aims to do and achieve. It should define your key activities and create an ethos or set of values which will govern how and what you do.

Sample mission statement

POP – Providers for Older People – is a charity which aims to serve the needs of older people in our local community by providing a meeting place and transport facilities.

We endeavour to help older people through our committed and dedicated team of volunteers, using wisdom and kindness, and exercising good management of the resources entrusted to us.

We wish to be known for delivering a quality service through caring for individuals.

Some mission statements are produced in isolation by one person, and are then agreed by everyone else within the organization. The most effective statements are created when everyone who has an active role to play in the organization – the chairperson and the office typist, the full-time staff and volunteers – is involved in the

Having a mission statement will reassure you that all your fellow workers are playing the same tune!

process and can feel genuinely committed to the finished article. This is often referred to as 'ownership'. It will be the task of one person to produce the final statement that takes into account the views of all those who contribute to the organization.

Ultimately, the most important thing about your mission statement is that it is understood by everyone, and is used to define and set the parameters for every day-to-day activity within your organization. As a fundraiser you need to know exactly what your organization stands for and what it is trying to achieve, so that you can tell potential donors.

Undertaking a SWOT analysis

A **SWOT** analysis is a simple tool that will help you to identify where you stand as an organization, particularly in relation to your 'competitors' for funds. Quite simply you consider your **strengths**, **weaknesses**, **opportunities** and **threats**, listing all the relevant points that you can think of under each heading.

Sample SWOT analysis

The Wacky Youth Project

Strengths	**Weaknesses**
Motivated volunteers	Local council disapproval
Lively, active participation	Local community disapproval
Bright, spacious hall	Short-term agreement for use of hall

Opportunities	**Threats**
New, younger mayor	Lack of income and support!

You may, for instance, consider the contacts of your chairman, the emotive quality of your project and the number of volunteers at your disposal to be great assets and so list them under 'strengths'. You may list your financial controls, and poor office equipment as 'weaknesses'. A new company setting up in the offices next door could be passed as a major 'opportunity' and a competing charity expanding its fundraising efforts could be included under 'threats'. Whatever the results, the exercise will help you to identify areas for attention to strengthen your position ready for fundraising.

Preparing a 'case for support'

Once again, this exercise is as valuable as the end result because it will make you take a critical look at the project or cause for which you are seeking funds. If there are problems or inconsistencies you should tackle them now – before you ask others to commit money or other resources to you.

The case for support is a brief document that presents your charity, project or cause to potential donors. It should define the needs of the organization or project for which funds are sought and offer reasons why it is worthy of support. It may also list influential donors who have already committed funds or other resources. Like the mission statement, all staff and volunteers should have copies of this document and understand it in every detail.

Sample case for support

Kidley-on-Sea Parent Teachers Association wishes to provide the best possible educational opportunities for children at Kidley-on-Sea Primary School. While the school provides admirably for the day to day needs, care and basic education of the children, we believe that we can enhance these efforts by funding further facilities.

In particular we feel that we can extend the children's physical development, provide for their safety and encourage their self-confidence by building and maintaining a swimming pool on site. Unfortunately, the school is no longer able to offer swimming lessons at the local sports centre because of transport difficulties. As ours is a seaside town we believe that we must teach our children to swim.

We need to raise £20,000 for the initial construction of the pool which will be undertaken at cost by our local firm Winning

Pools Limited. Plans are available for public inspection in the school office. We must find a further £1,500 annually for maintenance.

Already we have received a generous donation from local businessman, Ken Grantly, and Kidley's own Olympic swimmer, Bette Diver, has offered to front our campaign. The children themselves are determined to contribute and have formed their own fundraising committee under the leadership of brothers, Sam and Guy Goody. Even if you do not have a child at the school please join our efforts to provide a stimulating and safe future for the children of our town. PTA chairman, Chris Goody, can be contacted through the school for further information.

Developing a donations policy

In the first flush of enthusiasm for your project you will dream up countless schemes for tapping funds. Some of these will be your best ideas and you should pursue them with great energy and commitment. Some of them will be your worst – possibly because the donor is inappropriate. It is far better to decide at this stage whether you will take money from anyone, or whether there are some 'no go' areas. There is nothing more soul-destroying than to swing a deal for a good-sized donation and race back to the office to tell your colleagues, only to find that they don't approve of your donor.

You should, therefore, consult everyone whose view will matter – staff, volunteers, important supporters or grant-making bodies, trustees and committee members – to decide on a donations policy. There are some cases where it would be perfectly acceptable to take funding from any source and you may be one of the lucky ones. But your cause may be a particularly sensitive one. You may court very negative publicity, and even lose support, if you accept money from a source that others consider to be inappropriate.

If, for example, your charity supports the victims of cancer you may be well-advised not to take money from the tobacco industry. If you are fundraising for a school you might not wish to court the support of your local off-licence. And any organization might be wary of a donation from a public figure living in disgraced or colourful circumstances who might simply be image-building at your expense. These cases will be few and far between but it is important to think about them before you solicit funds.

In some cases a donation might seem inappropriate on the surface but further thought will justify it. If you find yourself in this position, be clear about your rationale and explain it to all concerned parties, including the press and the general public, if necessary. Be sure that your arguments will hold water and that the donation is worth the effort you take to justify it.

Case study

A company that used live rhinos in its advertising made a link with a wildlife protection charity in a joint promotion. There was a public outcry at this commercial exploitation of an endangered species by a wildlife organization. The charity explained that it was working with the company behind the scenes to improve the way the animals were treated and to make sure that the animals used had been captive bred and not taken from the wild. It would not have achieved this position of influence if it had not embarked on the promotion. Some, but not all, critics were silenced.

Remember, it isn't just the documents that you produce that are important to your future fundraising efforts. It is also the process of focusing your mind and your colleagues' minds on essential issues before you ask others to support you.

Sample donations policy

At POP – Providers for Older People – we wish to be open to the community around us. We are fundamentally a part of the community, and without the support of the community we would be unable to carry out our mission.

We would, therefore, wish to accept donations made by any local individual, statutory, social or corporate body that wishes to help us as part of a community effort. Currently we do not believe that a gift from any of our neighbours would cause us any embarrassment.

This policy applies purely to charitable donations. We do not expect to receive donations where there are conditions attached, but we would review this policy should such circumstances arise. We would also review our policy if a gift were offered from an organization outside our local area. It is unlikely that we would reject such an offer unless it came from a company operating in the defence business in which case we would decline the offer on moral grounds.

Questions and answers

Knowing your own organization

Q *My partner and I set up our charity several years ago. While we were fully agreed then about its aims we have diverged in our thinking about where it should go now. Should we take professional advice?*

A That, of course, is one option. You could call in a fundraising consultant or agency to give you a professional perspective, if you can afford it. Or you could canvas the opinion of others you know and trust. Try talking to those closely involved with your work, but maybe also with others who can stand back and give you a totally unbiased view.

The one certainty is that you must resolve your differences before you ask others to support your work with either their time or money. When you are clear about the way forward commit to it in a mission statement and work out a strategy that will achieve your goals over, say, the next three to five years. Don't attempt to fundraise until this crisis is fully resolved.

Changing a name

Q *The chief executive of the charity I work for wants to change our name to something 'snappier' and more memorable. He thinks our current name is a major weakness. We use a set of initials and I know these are boring but at least our supporters recognize them. What do you think we should do?*

A If in doubt don't! There are some valid reasons for changing a charity's name, say, for example, that your set of initials is being used by another organization. It may be that this other organization is using your name illegally and that you could fight against it in the courts, but it may also be that the value of the name is being eroded and you would do better to change it.

On the whole changing a name for the sake of it simply brings a raft of other problems. However hard you try to promote the new name you may never lose the old one completely, leading to an identity crisis. Confusion over who you are could lead to a drop in revenue. Simple things, such as finding your number in the phone book, become more difficult for potential and existing supporters. Some donors may think you have disappeared completely.

Even some of the best known charities have regretted a name change. If your existing name isn't memorable try to support it in other ways. If you don't already have a logo try developing a really powerful image to use alongside your name. Or try a catchy strapline. Use the press and promotional techniques explained later in this book to build awareness of your existing name and what it stands for. I hope you will be able to persuade your boss that changing the name isn't the only way to fix your charity in people's minds!

Taking money from 'unethical' sources

Q *I think my charity should take money from any source. Surely what matters is not where the money comes from but the use to which it is put. What better use can there be for 'dirty' money than for charities to use it in a really positive way? My colleagues, however, think we should turn down a donation that has just been offered by a tobacco company. What should we do?*

A The most important thing is that you come to an agreement within your organization before you do anything else. This situation may well arise again and it is best to be prepared. So work with everyone whose view will matter to develop a 'donations policy' that is mutually acceptable.

There are a number of factors to consider. Firstly what is ethical? Obviously you disagree on this but you must find common ground. Discuss your opinions rationally with your colleagues. Next, what sort of cause do you promote? If you are a children's or health care charity it may be particularly difficult to accept money from the tobacco industry. Think about the effect this donation may have on other valued supporters or donors. If they will be upset by the link with a tobacco firm it might be counter productive to accept it anyway. Might acceptance of the donation court negative publicity that would outweigh the value of the gift? Is the money a gift or are there strings attached?

When you have considered all these factors you must decide amongst you whether it is sensible to take the money or not. Make sure that everyone involved supports the final decision and produce a written document that makes your stance clear. You must be able to explain your policy to anyone who asks, so be sure of the rationale for your position.

Tackling weaknesses and threats

Q *It's all very well recognizing weaknesses and threats – but how do we do something about them?*

A Every organization will have to tackle its own problems. At least recognizing that these exist is part way to solving the difficulties they pose. Look at your own particular weaknesses and believe that you can do something about them.

If, for example, your problems are to do with staffing and manpower, a lack of skills or knowledge, you may be able to resolve them by recruiting additional staff or volunteers. Or it may be that existing staff could be trained to cover these areas of weakness.

Perhaps your weaknesses are more to do with attitudes and habits. These can be changed, so work with the others around you to find common ground and agreement about the way forward.

Maybe outside influences are impacting on your business. Search for a way to shift the balance in your favour. If, for example, another charity is stealing your thunder by attracting more publicity and support, consider a partnership with that charity. Or develop your own unique activities and events that will attract a completely new base of support.

There are always ways to resolve difficulties and to combat weaknesses. Be positive and proactive about them.

5 | 'MARKETING' YOUR 'PRODUCT'

Although many people in non-profit organizations are uncomfortable with the concept, the process of fundraising is, essentially, that of 'selling'. A charity 'sells' its cause or project to its donors or 'customers'. Even when altruism is the only motivation for the gift of funds and nothing is expected in return, the process of persuading the donor to give to your cause in preference to any other is selling. And, as that is the case, it makes sense to use the most effective tools of the sales trade to enhance your fundraising efforts.

Marketing is the process that professionals use to back up their sales efforts. In business terms, marketing identifies the right product, at the right price and promotes it to the marketplace. The **four ps**, as they are called, of **product**, **price**, **promotion** and **place** are referred to as the 'marketing mix'. Careful planning to get each of these 'right' is the secret of success. The conditions are different for charities, of course, but the four ps are still highly relevant.

What is your 'product'?

The most successful companies create products – jam jars, chocolate bars, motor cars etc. – specifically for their 'markets' or customers. They identify needs or gaps in the marketplace that other products do not fill. This is called 'making what you can sell, not selling what you can make'. In the charity world we often have to work the other way round and sell something that has been made already. Our 'products' are our projects and causes. Many will have been created to meet the needs of those who will use them – not those who will fund them. And it may not be in our power or remit to change them.

A fundraiser has to 'sell' the cause and the projects.

If, however, you are in the position of starting a charity or launching an appeal from scratch you may be able to apply a little marketing thinking to the product you are creating. Ask yourself if there really is a need for the project or service. When you are satisfied that there is, consider whether a base of support exists for it. Will you be able to 'sell' this particular concept or does it, by nature, pose difficulties? Are there sources of funding that you can tap and will they be responsive to the product you have to offer?

The answers to some of these questions may become apparent only as you start to fundraise, but it is better to research and answer as many of them as you can before you spend time and effort asking for money. If you have a project that no one will want to fund perhaps you should rethink your project, or at least its presentation. It is not that the tail should wag the dog – just that you should be aware of things donors are likely to support. As far as possible, you should ensure that your product appeals to them and is, therefore, 'fundable'.

If the project or cause for which you are to fundraise is up and running already, you will not have much influence on its essential characteristics, and you may start at a disadvantage. Your customers do not need your product, although they may gain a benefit from being associated with it. What you can, and should, do is to package your product to enhance that benefit.

Adding value for your donors

Taking a mundane item such as a diary and turning it into a desirable or even covetable product such as a Filofax or, to take it a step further, a Psion personal organizer, is called product development. A basic concept is enhanced, features and benefits that will appeal to the customer are added, and it is branded and packaged attractively and at a price the customer can afford. Within reasonable bounds the same process can be applied to charity projects.

The first step is to identify a discreet project for funding. Focus on what you need and divide your organization's work into self-contained sections. It is easier and more effective to tackle each one individually.

The local church, for example, might need a new set of bells, a set of new hymn books and funds for routine maintenance. As fundraiser you could, of course, put all these into one pot and set up 'The All Saints Appeal', but you will be much more effective if you divide your campaign. Each project should be set up in its own right, with its own need and target, and its own features or benefits to donors. You can aim each project at a different type of donor to secure funding from as many sources as possible.

The second step is packaging your product to maximize its appeal. Under the banner 'Ring in the New Year', the campaign to raise funds for the new bells could be targeted at the local business community. After all, this will be an expensive project and company budgets may be a better source of income than the purses of your congregation or parishioners. Set your target (the funds required) and construct your case for support – why the church needs new bells and what they will add to the local community. If you are going to approach companies for funding, think what extra benefits you could build into the project for them. The company's name could be inscribed on each bell for posterity. Perhaps a special peal could be created for the sponsor to be rung at an inauguration ceremony attended by local dignitaries and the press, of course. In this way you add value to your basic proposition and create a product that a local business might well want to buy.

The hymn books might better be funded by individuals in the congregation. 'Sing for All Saints' might be a more personal appeal. Set your target in terms of the number of books needed and aim for each individual supporter to 'buy' or cover the cost of one book. Explain the need for the new books to your target donors. You may find that not all the congregation will be purely altruistic so add a benefit for them. Try inscribing the name of the donor in 'his' book for all his peers and future users to see.

In each of these examples a separate 'product' has been identified and packaged to appeal to a carefully targeted group of donors. The chances of fundraising success will be far higher at All Saints now that the campaign to meet each individual need has benefited from a touch of marketing technique. And the fundraiser will have more fun, which means that he or she will be more motivated, which means more success – which is good news for all concerned!

Case study

A small charity produced nothing except a handbook to advise and support parents of children with a particular terminal disease. The fundraiser for the charity found it hard to ask for funds for a handbook – such a mundane product on such a depressing subject.

A donor then suggested that she should put the children and their parents up front. The fundraiser repackaged her fundraising material with pictures and stories about the children first, and the value of the handbook second. She nearly doubled her income.

Packaging a project to make it appeal to your potential donors is quite an art – and one that takes practice. Make sure that you think of all the different elements that belong to your project, including all your core costs, running costs and staff time, and build these in to your target. Search for the most unusual or appealing aspect of your project, and enhance it with a little creative thinking if need be. As with the church bells, decide what sort of donor will be most motivated by the project you are creating, and add in some extra elements just for them.

Covering costs

If adding benefits for donors costs a little more, don't be put off. You will need to spend money to raise money. It all should be in proportion and within reason, of course, and you should be able to cover these costs by building them in to your fundraising target.

In the case of the church bells, potential corporate sponsors should be presented with the costs that cover the entire project – purchasing and installing the inscribed bells, commissioning a special peal (if that carries a cost), staging an inauguration ceremony, producing materials for the press, and all the time and administrative costs of running the fundraising project.

Knowing your 'customers' and your marketplace

Chapter 7 will look in detail at different sources of funding, but at this stage it is helpful to recognize the importance of researching those sources and targeting specific products or projects at carefully chosen potential donors. This is the second 'p' – the place from which funding may come. Your chances of reaching your fundraising targets will be greatly increased if you aim the right products at the right marketplaces.

The fundraising task becomes much easier if you start to identify specific reasons why specific groups of people would be interested in your specific project. If you think simply of the general public as your donors you will find it hard to know where to start. If you segment that great mass of people and focus on the ones with particular reasons to give, the task will become more manageable – and you will be much more successful.

Case study

A small charity set up to fund projects for children in need in
South Africa had its administrative office in Wales. A special
corporate fundraising event had been planned at the South
African embassy in London. Who should be invited? Companies
local to the Welsh office did not want to travel to London for the
event. Interested parties in South Africa were unlikely to attend.
Few London businesses had any reason to be involved – those
with South African or Welsh connections were the best bet.

In the end a completely new audience of companies was created
by enhancing the event. Rugby was identified as a common
theme between the key nations. One of the key players from the
World Cup-winning South African team was invited as a
celebrity guest. He was also a charismatic team member of a
major London rugby club. All the many corporate supporters of
that club suddenly were relevant for the guest list. Welsh rugby
officials became involved too and again opened the way to more
companies.

Setting a price

Your fundraising target is, effectively, the price of your product –
the third 'p'. Obviously the price must reflect the costs of
production, so all your time and administrative expenses should be
built in. Having said that, the price must also be right for the
purchaser and so should reflect what you may realistically achieve
in terms of donations. If your planning and research have been
effective you will find a donor who will pay the full price for your
product or project.

Promotion

Because promotion, the fourth 'p', is so important to fundraisers, it
is covered in detail in the next chapter.

Questions and answers

Starting a charity that has little popular appeal

Q *I want to start a wildlife hospital for animals that have been injured on the roads. All of my family and most of my friends think I'm mad and say that no one will give me money for it. What should I do?*

A Maybe the first thing to do would be to try to persuade your family and friends of the merits of your idea. This will be a valuable exercise for you. Gather together all the arguments in favour of your plan and anticipate the arguments that they will make against you – and how to counteract those. Think about the need for the hospital, how and where it will be run and by whom. Where will your patients come from and what care will they need? Will you need a license or other formal permission? Do you need any qualifications? Consider how you will promote the hospital. Estimate the costs of your operation and who might fund it. In effect you will be putting together a simple business plan.

Friends and family might not be the best judges of your ideas so also try presenting your plan to several other people locally whose opinion you trust. You need to be sure that you can run your hospital efficiently and that it will be viable. If you won't be able to raise sufficient funds to run it properly then you may do better not to start it. Maybe you could find another wildlife organization in which you can become involved.

If, however, you can persuade others to support you, if your ideas are workable and if your own enthusiasm is undiminished, then you will be in a strong position to give your plan a try. Use this book to prepare everything thoroughly. Good luck!

Creating or embellishing projects to raise funds

Q *Surely it can't be right to create projects in order to raise funds?*

A Every charitable project should be driven by need and created in order to meet a need. Raising funds is subsidiary to that basic principle. But there are ways of making an essential project more attractive to donors and we, as fundraisers, should not shy away from this. Keep track of any costs involved. Make sure that they are justifiable and will bear scrutiny.

Getting to grips with sales and marketing

Q   *I feel really out of my depth when people talk about 'sales' and 'marketing'. How can I avoid making a fool of myself?*

A   For a start don't under-estimate yourself. I'm sure you will have sold something of your own before – a car, or a pushchair, or an unwanted piece of furniture. I expect you decided on a price for the item, described it in an advertisement that you put in a shop window or in the local paper to attract someone to buy. I bet you thought about the best features of your car, or pushchair or furniture – for example, low mileage or very good condition.

What you were doing, of course, were marketing and selling. There really is no mystique. All you need to do is to develop those activities of setting a price, describing and maybe enhancing your 'product', drawing attention to it and choosing a place in which to advertise. You have already covered the key aspects of marketing and selling. This book will help you to apply your own experience to the task and explain the key techniques and jargon that the professionals use.

Broadening your base of support

Q   *My voluntary organization has traditionally relied on membership income. Should we try to broaden our base of support and break into new 'marketplaces'?*

A   It is sensible to have a broad base of support. If you rely too heavily on one source of income you will be in great difficulty if that source should dry up.

It is vital, however, that your attempts to open up new income streams should be carefully planned and targeted. Think about your project and the type of donor it might attract. Then consider the range of ways in which you could reach those people and motivate them to give.

It may be that you could persuade your existing members to give more to you by offering them other benefits beyond membership – the chance to attend functions organized by you or to buy simple merchandise such as calendars or diaries, sweat shirts or T shirts branded with your name or logo. Perhaps you could open up completely new 'marketplaces'. It might be appropriate to apply for a grant from a local trust or to seek corporate sponsorship. Use Chapters 7 and 8 to help you identify sources of income and techniques for tapping them that are appropriate to your own situation.

6 THE NEED FOR PROMOTION AND COMMUNICATION

If there is one maxim that applies to fundraising, it is that you cannot fundraise in a vacuum. You need to create awareness of your product or project before you ask for money. Fortunately there is a wealth of promotional and communications techniques that any organization can use to influence public opinion and fly the flag for your cause. **Promotion** – the fourth 'p'- is vitally important.

If no one has heard of you, you can't expect anyone to give to you.

At the most basic level you will give your organization a name, perhaps a logo and values that others will always associate with it. You are starting to build a 'brand'. Your brand image must be honest and truthful so that you do not fundraise under false pretences.

Case study

One of the world's strongest brands – competing with mega brands such as Coca-Cola – is the Red Cross. The Red Cross name and symbol are instantly recognizable and instantly associated with a set of carefully cultured values. Because it is so well known and respected, the organization attracts support. It fundraises, extremely successfully, on the back of the image it has promoted. It's good to think that even in this incredibly commercial world, where millions of pounds are spent trying to build brand images, a charity is one of the leading players. Inspiration to us all!

Promotion is a vast subject. This chapter will look at the range of techniques available to you and focus on the importance of getting your promotion right by selecting appropriate techniques. When you have chosen the promotional activities that best suit your needs, you should deliver them according to a carefully constructed plan that will pave the way for your fundraising efforts.

As with any other plan or strategy this should start by defining your aims and objectives. It should encapsulate the message or messages that you wish to put across and select the audiences you wish to reach. It will identify the methods that will best suit your purposes and put all of this, tightly costed, into a realistic timeframe. If you need further help on planning, look at Chapter 10 which includes a sample promotional plan, and which explores the whole planning process in more detail through the development of the fundraising strategy. Exactly the same principles apply here.

Promotional materials

Every fundraising organization needs to have at least one or two simple promotional materials at its disposal. There must be some standard, but carefully produced, documents that you can give to potential donors. At the most limited end of the scale you should have your mission statement and the 'case for support' for your organization or project. However, you might have the resources and the need to produce much more complex documents, such as an annual report or a regular newsletter. You may even be in a position to produce a video or website. The important thing is to produce only what you need to achieve your organization's aims and objectives.

What do you need?

Far too many charities rush to produce glossy brochures that then sit packed in their boxes gathering dust, simply because nobody stopped to think whether they were really needed or who they were for. Assessing the need is the first step towards effective communication with your donors. Dividing the various promotional tools into groups that are broadly speaking 'essential', 'valuable', 'desirable' and 'in the realms of fantasy' may help you to establish what you must have.

THE NEED FOR PROMOTION AND COMMUNICATION

Essential

Here you should consider:

- a name – if you don't already have an attention-grabbing one
- a mission statement – carefully thought through and presented
- a case for support – as above.

These will tell your donor who you are, what you are seeking funding for and why. They are the most basic tools at your disposal and should be used by everyone in your organization when approaching donors. They may also be useful for giving to journalists and other people of influence to make sure that the message coming out of your organization is strong and consistent.

Office copies that will receive particularly heavy use might be best laminated. Otherwise there is no need for a lavish production – so long as the message is clear.

Valuable

Some of these tools will help you to establish a presence and start to create the branding for your project or organization that will be recognized by the audiences you wish to influence. Many of them are simple to produce and will not absorb too much of your valuable resources – time and money. But do think if they will genuinely enhance your case:

- **Logo** – keep the design clear, simple and relevant.
- **Strapline** – this should be short, simple and unambiguous.
- **Letterhead** – use your logo and strapline on this.
- **Compliment slips and business cards** – as above.
- **Fax header sheets** – if your logo is simple it will work better in black and white.
- **Fact sheets** – simply produced on a word processor these are useful if you have several different projects, or if the status of one is constantly changing. They should offer more detailed but relevant information to donors.

- **Leaflets** – these could be desktop published or may move into the realms of printed material. They are useful if you need to use diagrams or illustrations to explain or enhance your case.
- **Posters and fliers** – creativity is more important than quality of production – you must grab attention; you won't have space for many words and your posters and fliers will have to compete with many others.
- **Visual aids for presentations** – these can be anything from slide shows for the Women's Institute through to computer generated presentations for corporate fundraising approaches. Cut your coat to suit the cloth and make sure that your presentations are suitable for each target audience.

Try not to place your posters where they will cause a road accident!

Desirable

As your organization becomes more sophisticated you will probably approach donor groups, for example companies, that are more sophisticated in their own use of promotional materials. Here it may not be out of place to offer a glossier production, but take care not to go over the top. Not all of these materials need be printed. Some could be produced as audio or video cassettes. Use whichever suits your communication needs and your resources:

- **Brochure** – this is a more complex fundraising tool. In some instances you will be expected to produce a printed, probably colour, brochure, but beware of spending too much and putting off donors who think you cannot really need their charity. Take care not to make your brochure 'too finished' so that it looks like an end in itself. It should support your fundraising efforts and inspire others to give to you, so think carefully about who it is aimed at and what you want it to achieve.

- **Newsletter** – this may be vital for keeping a large supporter base informed and motivated. A newsletter can be as simple or as complex as you like and can afford, but remember that it is there to do a job, so define its purpose and target audience carefully before deciding on your presentation style and budget.

- **Annual report** – if you are required by law to produce an annual set of accounts, you may wish to incorporate this information into a more glossy annual report. Use this as an opportunity to communicate key messages with a specific target audience. If you are going to this expense, make the document really work for you – avoid the temptation of producing an annual report for the sake of it.

- **Website** – likewise this should serve a genuine purpose. Use it to communicate key messages to a computer literate audience. It may be particularly relevant if your donors are young or business orientated.

In the realms of fantasy

If you believe a video or a website could be yours only in your wildest dreams, that is exactly where it should stay. Do not aspire to things for the sake of them. If they would make a fundamental difference to your fundraising ability then they belong in another category – and you will find a way of funding them cost effectively.

Case study

A fundraiser for a smallish charity had some success in securing corporate funding. He believed that he would be still more effective if his presentation style were more professional. He persuaded one of his existing corporate partners to sponsor a laptop computer and Powerpoint software package so that he could run computer-generated presentations. The sponsor was given full credit in the presentation, which enhanced the sponsor's image with peer group companies and gave credibility to the fundraiser's sales pitch. With increased confidence the fundraiser achieved more than double his target.

Generating a house style

If you wish to look professional, all your documents should look as if they have come from the same organization. Make prominent use of your logo on every piece of printed material, and design a standard layout for letters and documents, choosing a single typeface to use on every occasion. Only change this on those special occasions when you are looking for a major, attention grabbing impact.

It is wise to channel the production of all promotional materials through one source. One person in your organization should be responsible for coordinating a house style that everyone uses, and it should be applied to letter writing as well as to the more complex design tasks. Using a single style and a single logo will reinforce your message in the marketplace and leave no room for confusion. It is all part of creating a respected brand.

The design of your logo, the choice of typeface and the type of paper you use will all say certain things about you. Use this to your advantage to create an image of your organization that is professional, contemporary – or whatever else you wish it to be.

Basic promotional techniques

Once you have a portfolio of promotional materials you can start to use them wisely. Each one should have been designed to meet a specific purpose and with a specific target audience in mind, so in some cases you will simply need to get on with the distribution. This can be by hand, through outlets such as your local library or supportive shops, or possibly by mail. We will look at the very specific skill of direct mailing in Chapter 8.

There is, however, a great deal more to promotion than simple distribution of leaflets. Everything you do should be planned to support your fundraising efforts, especially the timing of everything from leaflet distribution to press advertising. Take time to construct a promotional plan that will dovetail with, and support, your fundraising strategy.

Choosing the most appropriate method for your message is not always easy. Hone down your options by asking yourself what you want to achieve, who you are trying to reach, how quickly you need to do it and how much money you can spend in the process. Select the promotional activities that will meet your criteria. Usually a range of different techniques will achieve the best effect.

Advertising

Although one of the more expensive tools, there is a place for advertising in many promotional plans. Even the placement of a recruitment advert is an opportunity for brand building with considered use of your name, logo and house style and a few choice words about your organization and its objectives. Television, radio, cinema and national newspaper advertising may be out of your reach financially and will almost certainly demand the skills of an outside agency. Advertising in local freesheets or paid-for newspapers can be quite cheap and you can create the adverts yourself.

If you are designing the advert yourself, make sure that it stands out from the rest. You can use the **AIDA** formula to keep yourself focused. AIDA stands for:

Attention
Interest
Desire
Action

Your advert should grab **attention** and develop an **interest** in your subject. It should create a **desire** to be involved, and must prompt **action**. A picture is often more powerful than words.

One of the benefits of paid-for advertising is that you can usually be quite specific about the timing and, on the whole, adverts can be produced quickly to meet an urgent need.

Exhibitions and road-shows

Take your message to others with an exhibition or road-show. These will have longer 'lead' or development times and so should be planned further ahead. They can also carry considerable costs – especially if your displays are professionally produced and mounted, and if you have to pay for an exhibition space or a road-show vehicle. But it is possible to create a DIY version which, if costed and targeted carefully, can be a very effective way of promoting your message. To keep costs to a minimum you can put on a promotional display at your own offices, at the offices of other supporting organizations and possibly companies, or at local events such as fetes and sporting fixtures. Just be sure that the audience is worth the effort.

Open days, talks and seminars

Bring others to you with an 'open day' if you have the space to do it. Build in static displays and informal discussions as well as workshops, talks or presentations about your work. It is more difficult to target an audience for an open day so they are best used when you wish to inform or influence a broad spectrum of the general public in your locality.

Talks and presentations can be taken out, of course, to other carefully targeted audiences and you may wish to speak at seminars run by other organizations. Developing a basic presentation that you can use in most venues, but which can be tailored to the needs of each individual audience, will save you time and effort.

Promotional give-aways

These can be useful for raising awareness of your name and logo if your budget will run to them, or if someone else will sponsor them. Try stickers, car stickers, bags, flags or balloons.

Basic media relations techniques

No successful fundraiser will ignore the power of the media to promote their cause – and so pave the way for fundraising approaches. Your own charity may have a dedicated press office with which you can work to raise awareness of your fundraising activities, but you may have to do all of this yourself. While some people can't wait to meet the press, others are terrified by the prospect. Usually this is because of an ill-founded fear of the unknown and an awe of the aura sometimes created by the media.

There is no mystique. Journalists, newspaper editors and programme producers are just people like you and me going about their chosen careers. They are professional communicators. If you know something that will interest their readers, listeners and viewers they will want to talk to you.

And there lies the secret of successful relations with the media – only to offer them 'stories' that are relevant, interesting and newsworthy for their audiences. Be scrupulously selective. Choose your message to suit your purpose and work out who will be most interested in publishing it.

In the rest of this chapter we will explore the basic principles of media relations, covering enough of the subject to help you approach the press if this will enhance your fundraising efforts.

Don't bombard your local paper with every piece of information in the hope that one day something will be printed.

Creating a communications strategy

As with all your other promotional and fundraising activities your communications with others should be carefully targeted, with a clear message and planned in advance. Too many charities get involved in 'reactive PR' – where a journalist (or a trustee, or a volunteer) rings up because they have heard a rumour concerning the charity and want to know more. The charity has to react rapidly, possibly to prevent a crisis, dropping all other important tasks. While it is impossible to prevent this sort of thing entirely it would be possible to manage it more effectively. Plan ahead, recognize what is going to be of interest to others and what will support your fundraising strategy, and then select appropriate channels for communication.

Chapter 10 explores the process of strategic planning in more detail and you can use the advice given there to prepare a communications strategy. It also includes a sample 'promotional plan' which you could use as a model for a communications plan.

How to present a story

There are two ways to approach a journalist – by personal contact such as a phone call or a meeting if you can achieve it, or through a 'press' or 'news release'. While your chances of success are much greater if you can develop a personal rapport with chosen journalists, you may have to communicate on paper. Technically, a press release is used for the printed media while a news release is aimed at the rest – radio and television – but, in practice, the terms are frequently interchanged. We will use the term news release to cover all media.

First and foremost make sure that the issue of a news release will support your fundraising efforts. As a fundraiser you should spend time with the press only if you have a specific objective in view, for example to alert potential participants to an imminent fundraising event. Then follow these simple rules to make your release professional and to help it reach its target effectively:

- The content must be **relevant** to the journalist you are approaching. Find a strong local angle if you are approaching the local media. Pull out the elements that are most newsworthy or exciting and make sure they are in the first paragraph. Keep your copy brief, informative and to the point.

- Make sure that your release arrives on time to **meet the deadline** of your chosen newspaper, magazine or programme. Some magazines work several months ahead while some programmes and newspapers are put together on a daily basis. You will need to research deadlines carefully to make sure that your story appears at a time relevant to your fundraising efforts.

- **Use headed A4 paper** so there is no doubt who the release is from. Double space and leave wide margins for editing. Use a single side only and make sure each release is dated. End your copy with the word ENDS to mark the end of copy for publication, and then add a name and contact number for the editor's use only. Make sure that the contact number is manned even out of office hours.

■ Make sure that your **release reaches the right person** – research the appropriate correspondent for your particular story rather than mailing it to the editor. Always follow it up a day or two later with a phone call to offer further information, interviews, photos etc.

Working with journalists

It is well worth building a relationship with one or two journalists who could be particularly helpful to you. Take time to read relevant papers or magazines and to tune in to appropriate radio or television programmes. Watch and listen for journalists who cover your sort of story. When you have identified someone who you think might be sympathetic to your cause, or who is showing an interest in your subject area, try to arrange a meeting to see if you can offer useful material. Informally over lunch or for a drink after work can be just as effective as formally in an office. If you can't secure a meeting, try offering some useful pieces of information over the phone to establish your credibility.

Always give your chosen journalist information that will enhance the article or programme. If you are an expert in your subject offer your comments or opinions. As your relationship develops you may find that your journalist will come to rely on you as a valued source of accurate information, and will seek you out!

Getting the message across

There is no doubt that the clearest message will attract the greatest support. While press and promotional work may be subsidiary to your fundraising task it is, nevertheless, a valuable tool in the fundraiser's kit bag. If you are able to paint a clear and vivid picture of your needs, fundraising itself will become much simpler. Those who don't prepare the way often pay a heavy price, leaving potential donors confused and unwilling to commit themselves.

Sample press release

[on headed paper and with date of issue]

CELEBRITY DAD TAKES PLUNGE FOR FUN!

Local pop legend, Adam Shout, will be taking the plunge for the charity known as 'FUN' on Saturday. Adam and his six-year-old daughter, Philadelphia, will be the first to jump into the pool at this summer's opening of the Lido to raise awareness of FUN.

'Of course, I have my own indoor pool at home,' commented Adam, 'but it's nice to help out a local charity – especially one that does such good work.' FUN (Fathers United for Nurturing) works to promote the involvement of fathers in the upbringing of their children. The charity believes that many of our social problems spring from the absence or low profile of the father figure in modern families. It encourages fathers to bond with their children by organizing fun events and activities for 'dads and kids together'.

Philadelphia said, 'I hope the water will be warm. If not I shall ask Daddy to take me to FUN's 4x4 FUN day on 1 June instead!'

Adam and Philadelphia will take the plunge at the Lido at 10 am on Saturday 4 May to open the pool for the summer season. Fathers and children are particularly welcome, and the management of the Lido has agreed to donate all profits from the first day's takings to FUN. The water temperature is expected to top 80 degrees!

ENDS

Further information: Eve Smiley, FUN Office, 21 Happy Street, Paterbury, Surrey GU0 000 . Tel 01483 000000.

Case study

A wildlife protection charity gradually metamorphosed over a period of years into an environmental organization. The change was logical as the wildlife could be protected only if habitats were also protected from environmental degradation. The charity changed its name to reflect its growing concerns, but it failed to communicate its new mission to its existing supporters and potential new donors, leading to confusion about its role and remit. Efforts to fundraise were greatly complicated and hampered.

Questions and answers

Using straplines

Q *What is a strapline? How can a strapline help and how can I decide on one?*

A A strapline comprises a few carefully chosen words that you attach to your organization's or product's name to enhance understanding or draw attention. For example, 'Heineken – probably the best lager in the world'. This clever strapline draws attention through the use of humour and plants a memorable idea about the product that is reinforced every time we read the brand name.

Think how you could use this to your own advantage. You don't have to be funny or clever but you can explain or reinforce a key message about your organization or project every time you use a strapline. So if your organization is called POP, which stands for Providers for Older People, you could use 'providers for older people' as your strapline. Or you might try 'caring for the elderly in our community' or some other succinct phrase that conveys a solid message about who you are or what you do and thereby increases awareness within your community.

Try a brainstorming session with your colleagues, friends or supporters to come up with a strapline that is relevant to your organization.

Setting up a website

Q *A friend of mine has offered to set up a website for my organization. I don't know much about the new technologies and am afraid that it will be expensive to set up and difficult to use. What should I do?*

A If you think that having a website will serve a useful purpose that could not be met in a cheaper or better way, it would be worth investigating further. Establish the benefit that a website could offer your organization and weigh it up against other promotional tools in terms of cost and effectiveness.

Generally a website need not be out of the reach of small organizations in terms of cost. Many small charities do already have them. Once set up they offer cheap, fast, and powerful communication with an ever increasing number of donors and potential supporters. Over the next five years more and more organizations will make having a website a priority. If you don't know much about the new technologies perhaps you could enrol on a course that would help you to understand and use them.

However enthusiastic you become about new technology, and websites in particular, you must be sure that your potential donors share your knowledge before you set up a website. Younger supporters will find this method of communication commonplace and may expect you to use it. If most of your targeted supporters are unlikely to be computer literate or to have access to the Internet you may do better to communicate with them through more conventional means.

Producing a brochure by committee

Q *Our charity has decided to produce a brochure. Should we delegate one person to do this or should our whole committee contribute?*

A Firstly, I hope that you have established a need for the brochure and a target audience for it!

Writing by committee is enormously frustrating. Of course, everyone will have something to contribute, but far better that one person researches and compiles ideas and produces a draft for your committee to consider and approve.

Getting the best out of press relations

Q *I don't trust our local newspaper to print the truth and nothing but the truth about our organization. Is it better to avoid contact with it altogether?*

A I would try the opposite approach. While you can never guarantee that articles about you will be accurate, or even fair, the best way to work against such negative publicity is to work closely with the press, feeding them factual, relevant and timely information about your activities. Try to get journalists on your side.

Try to cultivate a trusting relationship with the editor or a key journalist on your local paper. Invite him or her to attend your functions as a guest, offer to show him the work you do and send him information that will be of interest to his readers.

7 SOURCES OF FUNDING, RESEARCH AND DONOR MOTIVATION

Now we can start to get down to the nitty gritty of where you should look to fundraise. There are many sources but not all will be willing to give to your type of project. You may also find that the skills and resources required to tap certain sources are beyond you at this stage. But if you investigate carefully and are honest with yourself about what you can tackle, you should find the funds to meet your needs. A healthy organization will seek its income from a range of different sources so that it never relies too heavily on any one. This chapter investigates the major sources of funding, the pros and cons of taking money from each, and looks at the factors which induce each type of donor to give.

Researching potential donors

The key to successful fundraising is to ask the right person to give – the person who has funds available and who will be motivated by your cause or project. This process of 'targeting' appropriate potential donors can be more or less scientific. It can range from simple 'gut reaction' – perhaps in a local context where the fundraiser knows the pool of donors pretty well and uses that knowledge to target those most likely to give – to the use of formal research. Most of us will probably rely on both techniques, but the bigger and more ambitious the target you have set, the more likely you are to need to research new sources of funding.

However varied the sources from which you seek funds – whether individual or organizational, commercial or statutory – there are some basic questions you need to ask if you are to identify the best targets for your fundraising approaches.

First, is this donor in a position to give? If you are approaching a company, or a local authority, or a trust fund, does a budget exist from which a donation could be drawn? Is this the right time to apply to that budget and who controls it? If you are targeting a 'wealthy' individual are you sure that this person has disposable income? If not, you need to find another target!

Next, will this donor be motivated by your cause? Many companies, trusts, foundations and statutory organizations have policies which define the causes they are prepared to support. You need to know which might support you and which you shouldn't waste time asking.

Individuals, as we all know if we look at ourselves, are motivated by a host of factors that range from a general sense of compassion or concern through to a strong personal connection with the cause. The major national fundraising events such as Comic Relief and Children in Need rely heavily on the former. Vast sums of money are raised because ordinary people are made aware of the problems that face others in our world. These telethons raise our levels of compassion and heighten our concern. They bring to our attention desperate needs, of which we might otherwise be unaware. Add to that a touch of guilt, that these people are suffering while we live comfortably, and the emotive donation response is triggered.

In other cases it is a personal connection with the cause that motivates a donor to give. Of course, it is mostly parents and grandparents who will come to the school fete, and it is those whose close relatives or friends have suffered from diseases who will be most likely to support a research fund into that illness. The important thing is to work out who will be motivated by your cause.

Finally, what sort of approach will be needed to reach the donor? Does a company expect a formal presentation from the most senior person in your organization? Does a trust fund require all approaches for funds to be made on its own application forms? Will a wealthy individual give only through personal contacts? All this is vital information and needs to be researched if you are to keep your fundraising efforts relevant and effective.

Where to find information

There are plenty of places to look for background information. Local knowledge is, of course, important and the closer you can get to your community the better. Do this by 'networking' with other people – including those who work for other small organizations like yours if you can. Read the press, watch the television and listen to the radio to find out what other charities and companies are doing. Getting onto the mailing lists of other charities will keep you in touch with new fundraising ideas and initiatives. Then home in on specific donors and research their policies, procedures and attitudes by looking in the various guides to grant-making bodies, companies and wealthy individuals.

There is a wealth of directories and guides which will help you to identify potential donors. Some of the best are produced by the Directory of Social Change which will send you its catalogue of books free of charge (address in the Appendix). Don't feel that you have to spend a fortune on expensive books – even the most obscure publication can usually be sourced by your local library for a small fee. Many universities offer an 'open access' system to their libraries for reference, or you can join to borrow books for a fee. Local business schools and institutions may allow you access to their libraries if you ask them.

Then there is modern technology which, if you have access to it, can transform your research practices. The Internet itself is, of course, a fabulous research tool. At the touch of a button you have access to some of the most current information available from around the world on almost any subject you care to mention. For general information on fundraising try the websites provided by the Charity Commission, the National Council for Voluntary Organisations, Charities Aid Foundation and UK Fundraising (all addresses in the Appendix).

To research information on specific donors see if your targeted company or trust has its own website. The more professional your donors, the more likely they are to have websites that you can consult for essential information before making any approaches.

Case study

A good relationship with a business training centre can be a valuable asset in many ways. One small charity developed a rapport with a local business centre by asking to use the reference library. In this way the fundraiser was able to study books on marketing and promotion which helped with his approaches to companies.

One thing led to another as a good rapport developed between the two organizations, and eventually the charity was able to borrow meeting rooms and even held a fundraising 'Splash Day' at the centre's swimming pool!

There are also a number of computer data bases that can help you identify potential funding bodies. It may be worth asking your local Voluntary Service Council if they can help you to access these. Some of the databases are linked to the Internet while others operate off CD-ROMs and computer discs.

One of the best known is FunderFinder, which you can use to select information on relevant grant-making trusts. FunderFinder helps you to build a profile of your organization using tick boxes and menus. It then uses that information to filter out trusts that will not support you, leaving you with those that might. It also offers a free software programme that helps you to write your own grant application. Another package worth considering is Grantseeker from the Directory of Social Change. (See addresses and contact details in the Appendix.)

The rest of this chapter looks at different sources of funding, discusses which are appropriate for small voluntary organizations and examines the factors that trigger donations.

Statutory funding

Some fundraisers live in awe of the government institutions that could make them grants – and so they never apply. Certainly the range of grants and the bodies they come from is vast and it takes close investigation to home in on the appropriate ones. But statutory funding is not only valuable because of the income it offers – it also gives an informal endorsement which may encourage others to give. While results in this sector are never quick and easy, the benefits can be substantial.

Statutory funding is particularly valuable for some of the more obscure or less appealing causes which may be difficult to promote to the general public or to companies. As long as the project is valid and meets the criteria of the grant-making body, it will not have to be high profile or strongly motivating to a wide range of people.

The key bodies within the statutory field are central government, local authorities and health authorities. If your project is in the appropriate sphere you may also find funding through bodies, such as the Arts Council, set up by central government to promote a specific area of activity. And, if you meet its criteria, The European Commission may provide funds.

In favour of statutory funding are the following factors:

- Sizeable grants may be available.
- Implicit endorsement from a government body which may encourage others to give.

■ Support may be available for projects that are less appealing to other donors.

Against statutory funding are the following factors:

■ There are often lengthy application and decision-making processes.

■ Political factors that are beyond the influence of the fundraiser may impact on an application for a grant.

■ Restrictions on how the money can be spent may be imposed.

■ Detailed submissions may be required.

UK government grants

As government policy dictates a shift from the direct provision of services to a 'contracting out' culture, so the scale of government support to non-government organizations providing care in the community has grown. If your work is relevant to one of the government departments it would be worth further investigation to see if your organization might be able to access a grant – but the process will probably be slow and will be influenced by political factors. Government grants are given as a means of furthering government policy and are not made simply as a recognition of good work or a worthy cause. Unfortunately, there is no formalized system for accessing a government grant. Look in your telephone directory for the number of the relevant department, and follow the advice given by each individual department for making applications.

Local authority and health authority grants

As with central government there is now a heavier reliance on the contracting out of services, and you may find that your organization is awarded a contract rather than a grant. Again, your activities will have to be consistent with the policies of the local or health authorities if you are to qualify for support. You may find that you can access 'joint funding' from both local and health authorities where your project is relevant to both. Start with your telephone directory to identify the most relevant department, and follow through the process required by individual authorities for making applications.

Funding from the European Union

European Union funding programmes are agreed at Community level, but their practical implementation is usually the responsibility of national or local agencies. So you will need to approach the relevant UK government department in the first instance. Most grants relevant to UK voluntary organizations will be made through the European Social Fund which focuses on youth and employment, education and training.

A free leaflet called, 'Funding from the European Union', available from the NCVO (address and phone number in the Appendix) gives an overview of all possible sources and purposes of funds from the European Union.

Giving by companies

There is very little true altruism or good old-fashioned patronage left in today's commercial world. While many companies give to charities and some of the donations are huge, the motivation for such giving is mostly enlightened self-interest. Not that this need be a problem for fundraisers – just that it must be recognized if corporate donations are to be tapped effectively.

The background to company giving

Where once company giving to charities was largely unplanned and even at the whim of the chairman, charitable budgets nowadays have to work hard to achieve a business purpose. This sea change occurred in the 1980s when political thinking espoused the causes of self-interest and self-help. Businesses became sharper and more focused in their charitable giving to the point where most donations now are linked to a specific commercial aim or objective. Most commonly this aim is 'to be seen to be a good corporate citizen', but there is a multitude of business objectives, from promoting a specific brand's image right through to directly increasing sales, that has been achieved through joint activity with charities.

The down side of this is that those useful, chance donations from the chairman are much harder to find. But, equally, there are now enormous opportunities for forging partnerships with companies that work for the benefit of both parties. With careful planning and execution these can not only increase funding but also offer other advantages in terms of staff secondment, transfer of skills, gifts in kind and staff fundraising.

While often regarded, erroneously, as the universal panacea, funding from corporate sources can still be a useful string to the bow of many small organizations. As long as it is kept simple – with not too much asked and not too much expected in return – most charities could benefit from an injection of corporate funds.

Factors in favour of corporate funding are:

- There are often substantial sums available.
- A development of 'mutually beneficial partnerships' that offers more than just money is possible.

Factors against corporate funding are:

- A long lead time is often necessary.
- Securing the funding is often labour intensive.
- Business skills will be valuable, if not essential.
- There are usually strings attached.

Types of corporate giving

Most corporate giving comes from one of two key sources, which can broadly be termed 'charitable' and 'commercial'.

In the **charitable** bracket we would include donations from 'charitable budgets' and these represent the closest to an altruistic gift. But very few donations of this kind are made without an expectation of something in return, usually public recognition, and so will still come with some strings attached. Often a joint press release announcing the donation will be required. The company may be very specific about which projects it wishes to support and may require progress reports.

This is, however, the better source of corporate income for small organizations with few resources. If you want a company to take an advertisement in one of your publications or to sponsor a small event, this is the place to look. Large companies with many smaller local outlets, such as supermarkets, banks and building societies, often allocate small budgets for use at local level, given at the discretion of the local manager.

Usually the charitable budget is controlled by the Community Relations or Corporate Affairs section of a major company or by a separate Corporate Trust Fund. In some smaller companies charitable giving is controlled by the PR Department or the Managing Director's office. Do your research to find out which applies.

On the **commercial** side the income to the charity may well come from a marketing or PR budget. The project to be 'sponsored' or the joint activity to be run will be competing, as a promotional tool, with everything in the corporate promotions armoury from television advertising to on-pack promotions. It must prove its value in the sharpest commercial terms. If sponsorship of a particular charitable event or activity will not generate greater press coverage or increase sales as effectively as any other promotional technique, it simply will not happen.

This is not the place to look for funds if you do not have some business acumen and knowledge of the promotions business. Nor should you try to swing a commercial deal if you don't have skilled staff available to deliver your side of the bargain. Mostly this is the province of the bigger charities which have dedicated Corporate Fundraising or Business Development departments – but there will always be exceptions.

There are a number of other ways in which companies may give to charities which do not involve a donation of corporate funds. **Giving in kind**, **staff secondments**, **Give As You Earn** and **staff fundraising** can all make valuable contributions to small organizations. Normally the Personnel or Human Resources Department should be approached first for gifts of office equipment, although the Community Relations team may become involved if you are after something more substantial, such as a vehicle. The company is likely to want some public acknowledgement for a larger gift. This department would also be the first port of call for secondments of company staff to your organization, for the Give As You Earn scheme for employees, and any ad hoc staff fundraising on your behalf.

Why do companies give?

What motivates a company to give? Unless you are truly lucky it won't be simply a desire to help a good cause. If, however, you can find a way that genuinely helps a company to do any of the following you will be in with a good chance of securing a corporate deal:

- enhance corporate/brand image
- endorse a product or service
- increase sales
- increase awareness
- access mailing lists
- access celebrities
- access unusual venues
- access expertise.

Case study

A small charity that had little public recognition or support was able to secure a corporate sponsorship of £5,000 (which, in its turn, generated a further £20,000) by 'selling' one of its assets – access to a celebrity.

The charity was supported by a film star who had personal reasons for his involvement. He was prepared to open his country mansion home to the charity for a summer ball.

Attracted by the unique venue and the celebrity host, a company sponsored all the costs of the event which then generated £20,000 in ticket sales, raffle and auction takings. The company was able to entertain influential guests at the event and generated strong, positive PR through its association with both the film star and the charity.

Grants from trusts and foundations

Grant-making trusts and foundations are one of the most valuable sources of income for small organizations. They differ from every other source in one essential characteristic – they exist to give, and operate for that purpose with few distractions or conflicting needs. For this reason alone it is probably easier and less costly to fundraise from trusts than from almost any other source.

The number of trusts and foundations, the range of causes they support and the sums of money they distribute are substantial, which means there is a good chance that you will find one to support your work. Many trusts are very clear about the type of projects they will fund, and publish policies that save both grant maker and grant seeker considerable time and effort. Others are more obscure. Some of the smaller trusts confine their support to a limited geographical area, and so fit neatly with smaller, locally based voluntary groups.

Finding a trust to fit is the key to this form of fundraising. It may demand the dedication to detail and the persistence of a detective. It can be a time-consuming task – the research must be done to identify the trusts that may respond to your needs. There are, however, computer packages designed to do some of the searching for you, if you can afford to invest in them or can access them in some other way.

Fortunately, most of the sourcing work can be undertaken by one person at a desk with just one or two reference guides, so saving costs. If your targeted trusts are local, it is also worth developing personal contacts with the trustees to further understanding of your project or cause. Once again, who you know can be an important factor in securing a grant.

Perhaps the best news for fundraisers is that trusts and foundations are not governed by commercial necessities or political constraints. On the whole, they can give where they choose. There are rarely other outside factors that could count against you – except, of course, the competing interests of other charities. If the fit is right and the work of your organization meets the criteria of the trust, you will be well-placed to trigger a grant.

Because there are few outside constraints, trusts can afford to take risks with their grants and many will fund start-up operations. An appropriate trust will consider projects that might not easily attract support from other quarters and on the whole expect less recognition than, for example, a corporate sponsor.

Trusts and foundations – the background

A few of the oldest trusts and foundations go back hundreds of years. Many were set up by genuine philanthropists who saw the need for charitable giving in an era that preceded the welfare state. Often these earlier trusts were limited geographically because the need perceived by the original benefactor was a local one.

The number of trusts was counted in hundreds rather than thousands until Victorian philanthropy triggered the foundation of many more. These were often at the instigation of wealthy commercial families such as the Cadburys, a trend followed in the twentieth century by families such as the Sainsburys. The work of the Victorian trusts and foundations was frequently linked to relief of the poor. More recently the influence of appeals such as Comic Relief and Children in Need, and phenomena such as the Community Fund (previously known as the National Lottery Charities Board), have broadened the spectrum of grant giving to cover almost every aspect of charitable work.

How do trusts work?

Trusts and foundations are established through the creation of trust deeds that set out chosen charitable objectives, as well as the names of the original trustees and the initial assets. As trusts cannot change purpose without legal alteration of the trust deed, many register a very broad base of objectives so that they are not confined by original aims that may well metamorphose over time. They may, however, declare a very limited area of giving in their donations policies. These are the relevant indicators for fundraisers.

Trusts in England and Wales will be registered as charities with the Charity Commission, while those in Northern Ireland and Scotland are overseen by the Inland Revenue.

Some trusts are endowed while others fundraise to generate their assets. Each will have its own individual method of operation, although the larger trusts are usually run on business lines with paid administrative staff and a Secretary or Director who reports to the trustees. Some will publish their methods and purposes while others remain very private and obscure. The important thing is to research thoroughly the ones that will have an affinity with your project or cause and to focus your fundraising efforts on those.

Factors in favour of trust funding are:

- Trusts exist to give.
- Substantial sums are available.
- Start-up funds are available.
- Innovatory, experimental or otherwise unpopular projects may be eligible.
- The cost to you is low.
- Sometimes a little recognition expected, but this is usually less than a corporate sponsor would demand.
- Continued funding for several years may be possible.
- Less specialist knowledge is required to fundraise.

Factors against tust funding are:

- Decision-making can be slow.
- Detailed submissions may be required.
- Trusts usually give only to registered charities or those that can prove charitable purpose.

The Charities Aid Foundation (CAF) has a special role to play in the grant-making arena. It is a grant-making trust in its own right, using money it has raised by donations to fund charities with particular needs. Like many of the larger trusts, CAF uses independent experts to guide the distribution of around £400,000 every year. CAF also allocates much more on behalf of government, foundations, companies and other donors.

The subject of applying for a grant from any trust or foundation is covered in the next chapter.

Giving by individuals

Nearly 75 per cent of the British population claims to give regularly to charity. Giving by individuals is the mainstay of funding for many small organizations in the UK and will always be of vital importance to fundraisers. The key to successful fundraising in this area is to target those who will be motivated by your cause, to persuade them to give instantly and generously, and then to nurture their continued support over time. Far too many organizations ignore the last part of this exercise.

There are many ways in which individual donors 'do their bit' for charity. A guilty conscience can be eased by anything from buying a copy of the 'Big Issue' on a street corner or attending a charity ball, to manning a stall at the local fete or walking from one side of the country to the other with a full sponsorship sheet. The point is that donors don't only give money. They also give their time to make more money – and this habit can be used extremely effectively by fundraisers.

Motivation

It is unjust, of course, to suggest that we, as individual donors, are motivated only by a sense of guilt – the issue is much more complex than that – but it is true to say that degrees of guilt do influence many giving decisions. The fact is that we do live in an affluent society and many of us are touched by the plight of others less fortunate than ourselves. Many of us wonder what put us here, and others there. Why are we the lucky ones? Should we sit back and enjoy our privileges, or should we redistribute a little of our wealth?

Sometimes it's hard to say whether a donation has been triggered by genuine compassion and concern for a worthy cause, or perhaps by a little enlightened self-interest. When we give to cancer charities do we do so because we sympathize with the sufferers, or because we would like to see research into the illness advance … just in case?

These are issues that face us all on a daily basis and we develop responses to these questions which will influence our giving. Some will turn to a religious code to guide their conduct while others develop a more personal moral code. Some will simply bury their heads in the sand. What it means for fundraisers is that there are a myriad different reasons for giving – and so a myriad different ways of generating funds.

Emotions have a great deal to do with personal giving. It may just be the 'aahh' response generated by an image of a small wide-eyed child or a fluffy animal, or it may be a much deeper caring evoked when someone we know suffers from a particular illness or disease. Every emotion should be treated with respect, but it is also right and fair to use the emotive response to help fund worthy causes.

On a lighter note there are those who simply support a cause or a project because they have a personal interest in it – they might even get pleasure from it. Members of the local cricket team will be the first port of call for the fundraiser who has to finance the new pavilion!

Factors in favour of fundraising from individuals are:

- Funds are available to any small organization – charitable status is not necessarily required.
- Large sums are achievable.
- Funds are easily accessible.
- Response times are quick.
- Few specialist skills – but a lot of energy and commitment – are required.

Factors against fundraising from individuals are:

- Patterns of giving are hard to establish.
- Some donations are not traceable, and so not repeatable.
- The attitudes of some individuals are critical.

Attitudes to fundraisers and charities

The vast range of reasons for giving is matched by the vast range of attitudes to charities. Anyone who has tackled a door-to-door collection will have experienced every response from charm and generosity to downright aggression and rudeness. Of course, the chances of avoiding the latter are greatly enhanced by careful targeting of appropriate donors – but even the best fundraiser will find it hard to target a street collection effectively.

Common barriers to successful fundraising from individuals include the widespread belief that the welfare state should provide much of the care which is now the work of charities. Or, at the other end of the spectrum, the attitude that 'they should help themselves'. There is also an unhelpful cynicism that little of the money given will reach those for whom it is intended, and that charities spend far too much on administration and fundraising. The best we can do to combat these attitudes is to practise and promote the very highest of standards, and to explain that fundraising carries a cost.

Community funding

Apart from the four main sources of funds discussed so far – statutory funding, corporate giving, grants from trusts and foundations and individual donations – there are a range of other organizations or institutions that may be of great value to you. Community-based bodies ranging from scout groups to Townswomen's Guilds may provide funding or help you to fundraise.

This may not be a major source of income, but if you have an affinity with one of these groups or you can foster a good contact within one, there are many ways in which your efforts could be supported.

Types of bodies to consider are:

- Round Table
- Rotary Clubs
- Lions Clubs
- Inner Wheel
- Trades Unions
- Townswomen's Guilds
- Mother's Unions
- Women's Institutes
- Young Farmers
- Youth Clubs
- Scouts
- Cubs
- Beavers
- Guides
- Brownies
- Schools
- Pubs
- Shops
- Restaurants
- Churches
- Sports clubs.

Fundraising through community groups

The strength of these groups is that they can often mobilize significant numbers of keen volunteers to fundraise on your behalf or tap into a customer base or clientele that might not otherwise be accessible to you. As well as reaching other donors they can stimulate giving by adopting your charity as their chosen cause for a period of time. Many of them are seasoned fundraisers who will have invaluable knowledge of different fundraising methods and who will know what will work where.

If you don't have the manpower to do it yourself, these are the people who could help you to run jumble sales, car boot sales, coffee mornings, auctions, fun runs, sponsored walks/swims/bike rides etc.

By working with community groups you will learn from seasoned fundraisers.

Lottery funding

Which brings us – as the final section in this chapter on sources of funding – to the still controversial subject of lottery funding. There has been much heated debate about the National Lottery and its impact on charity fundraising. What cannot be denied is that numerous organizations have applied for and received Lottery Grants – a major boost to their fundraising efforts. Of every pound spent on the National Lottery around 28 pence goes to the 'good causes' defined by parliament, of which 'charities' is just one.

The Community Fund (previously known as the National Lottery Charities Board)

Since the first grants were announced in 1995, the National Lottery Charities Board, and now the Community Fund, has awarded more than 20,000 grants worth over £1 billion. It is the largest independent grant-making body in the UK and the biggest single source of voluntary sector funding after statutory sources. Whatever your moral view on the Lottery's impact, or on playing a lottery at all, it does make sense to consider this as another avenue for sourcing funds, but do watch for changes to systems and procedures in this very fluid area of fundraising.

The Community Fund sets out to improve the quality of life in the community and to help meet the needs of those at greatest disadvantage in society. It receives 4.7 pence from every £1 spent on the Lottery and distributes this to charities and voluntary and community groups. Your organization does not have to be a registered charity to apply for a grant.

The application can take time and effort which may not always be rewarded, and conditions, especially relating to matching funds, may be attached. The Fund has operated several different themed grants programmes. You should contact your regional office (numbers are listed in your phone book) to check current themes and whether your project would be eligible. Application packs can be obtained by phoning the application line or visiting the website. Addresses, phone numbers and website details are listed in the Appendix.

Other Lottery distributors

Besides the Community Fund, there are eleven other distributing bodies responsible for giving grants to sport, the arts, heritage, millennium projects, and health, education and the environment. They are the Sports Councils and Arts Councils of England,

Scotland, Wales and Northern Ireland, the Heritage Lottery Fund, the Millennium Commission and the New Opportunities Fund.

Recent rule changes mean that Lottery funds can be applied more broadly, to fund people as well as capital projects.

Factors in favour of Lottery funding are:

- Large sums are available.
- Charitable status is not necessarily required.
- The Lottery's broad themes are less limiting than many other grant-making bodies' criteria.

Factors against Lottery funding are:

- Sometimes the process from application to grant is lengthy.
- Sometimes strings are attached.

Questions and answers

Investing time in research

Q *I seem to spend an inordinate amount of time researching potential donors and sending out applications for very little financial return. Are there any short cuts?*

A Only you know how efficient you are being when you research and make applications for funds. Use this book as a guide to check your own practices.

The only short cuts are to use more modern technology to replace the hours spent working through guides to grant givers and acquiring knowledge about them. Thorough research is essential if the time you spend making applications for funds is not to be wasted. Bear in mind too that you are facing a good deal of professional competition for available funds, and so the more focused and professional your approach the more likely you are to succeed. Thorough preparation will pay dividends.

But don't be too hard on yourself either. You may have to make a hundred applications before you receive one positive response. Fundraising is all about hard graft and determination. Take comfort from the fact that the more experienced and professional you become the more effective you will be.

Formal contracts

Q *Raising money from companies worries me because of formal contracts. Do these always apply?*

A If you will be taking money from marketing, PR or advertising budgets then, yes, you almost certainly will be required to commit to a formal contract and you should be absolutely certain that you can deliver your side of the deal before you sign up. Even where there is no formal contract, an exchange of letters agreeing to a joint activity will be legally binding. So beware.

If you need help understanding a contract that is presented to you by a company, or with drawing up a contract yourself, do take professional legal advice. Try to find a solicitor who will give his services to you free or at a discount.

All your exchanges with your donors should be totally honest, thorough and professional. If this is always so then contracts should hold no fears for you. They are simply the legal expression of something that you will do in any case.

Confrontation on the doorstep

Q *The thought of someone being rude to me really puts me off doing door-to-door collections. Is there anything I can do about this?*

A You won't be able to change human nature and, unfortunately, you will never know if you are about to catch your targeted donor at a bad moment or in a really bad mood. You can minimize the risks of confrontation by collecting from areas where you know you are likely to have support. If someone is rude to you the best thing to do is to back off quickly and politely. Try not to take any unpleasant comments personally.

If you can't face this possibility try a street collection instead where you are on neutral territory and people who don't want to give are likely to ignore you. Or try organizing a fundraising event where everyone who participates does so because they want to. You should always match your fundraising methods to your own skills and resources. If handling confrontation is not one of your strengths try fundraising methods that you will be good at and will enjoy. Ultimately you will be more successful.

8 | FUNDRAISING TECHNIQUES

With such a range of sources of funding available there has to be a range of techniques, finely tuned over years of use, for accessing funds from each source. While there will always be new, creative and innovative variations – and just occasionally the emergence of a completely new method – the basic techniques do not change. You will be able to elaborate on or improvise with the ideas you find in this chapter. The aim is to show you the range of options that exists and to help you evaluate which will best suit your own purposes.

In each case we will explore the applications of each technique, the benefits it offers and the skills and resources required to carry it through. By the end of this chapter you should be able to make a rational and reasoned judgement about the methods you will use to reach your fundraising target.

Running a major appeal

Sometimes referred to as 'capital' or 'big gift' fundraising, this type of campaign will be run to secure a large sum of money for a specific project through a public appeal. There should be a very clear target and a defined end use for the money. Part of the technique may be to secure major gifts from private sources before the main appeal is launched to the public.

This is the sort of exercise that gets organizations noticed, so there could be benefits to be reaped in terms of recognition and a broader supporter base, as well as financial rewards. It is, however, a major undertaking that will require a substantial input of time, dedication and professionalism, possibly from a committee rather than one committed individual. Finding one or more major donors is a skilled task and should not be undertaken lightly. If you do decide that you have the time and resources – as well as an appropriate project on which to focus a campaign – these are the key stages that you will need to consider:

- choosing a focus
- planning the campaign and making sure it is feasible
- recruiting a management committee
- producing publicity materials
- seeking high-profile support and the 'big gift'
- launching the appeal
- running the appeal and keeping it alive
- reaching target and saying thank you.

The focus

This may be very obvious if, for example, you wish to raise funds for a piece of cancer screening equipment or a swimming pool for a school. If the focus is not immediately clear, question whether this is the best method of fundraising. Presentation is important and so are your powers of persuasion to convince others that this is a worthy cause.

The purpose of the appeal must be clear to all potential donors. If you do decide to launch an appeal to cover running costs you should not mislead the public into believing that the money will be used for something more specific.

The planning phase

You will need very sound planning skills to mastermind this sort of campaign. Your organization may need to commission a feasibility study from architects, surveyors etc. for the project to be funded and will certainly need to make sure that it is soundly costed. Planning the fundraising campaign itself, and working out who is going to do what and when, is a major task. You will need sound administrative back-up throughout (if you are not an admin person, make sure that you have someone on board who is) and a database of potential donors.

If possible, it is wise to set an end date for the appeal and to put in place contingency plans for any surplus funds. Likewise you should consider what you will do if insufficient funds are raised. You may have to return contributions made in good faith. The Charity Commission can give guidance on these issues.

Do make sure that you set up a sound accounting system for the appeal. It is probably best to organize a separate bank account for all incoming funds, and you should set up a system to keep track of your donors as far as you can.

The committee

You will almost certainly need varying skills (planning, finance, marketing, PR, networking and administration among others), probably from a number of different people, to make this technique work for you and it may be best to recruit a committee (see Chapter 3). If you think you are unlikely to find enough committed supporters, question whether you should use other fundraising methods that you can run yourself.

Publicity

The merits of your campaign will be told through the publicity you generate and the supporting materials you produce (see Chapter 6). To a large extent, success in fundraising will be dependent on the profile you manage to create for your appeal. You must be skilled in this area, or have access to someone who is, to be effective.

However tempting it is to be carried away with exciting ideas for publicity, you must be able to keep your feet firmly on the ground and to ensure that all descriptions of the appeal and projects to be funded are entirely accurate and truthful. Remember you have a duty not to mislead potential donors.

The 'big gift'

Professional practitioners would expect a major appeal to have generated as much as half of the target income before the appeal is ever launched. A great deal of networking and persuasion will go on behind the scenes to get an appeal up and running before the public launch. In the classic model, the 'pyramid of giving', one or two major donors will sit at the top of the pyramid while the base will be provided by a large mass of small donors. When an appeal

is launched it helps to have the 'big gift' already secured to motivate others. You will need both the skills and the contacts to attract substantial gifts, preferably from high-profile donors who will also lend their names to the appeal. This part of the process could be contracted out to an agency or consultant (see Chapter 3) if you can afford it and if you can be sure of their success.

The launch

The scale of the public launch must match the scale of the target. Assess whether your appeal would attract regional television coverage or whether local radio and newspapers will be more likely to cover your story. You will need to know how to handle the press (see Chapter 6).

Running the appeal

The appeal itself may run for some length of time and you will need to find ways of keeping it alive with new initiatives to generate the target income. You may use many of the other techniques discussed in the rest of this chapter as part of your major appeal.

Reaching your target!

When you reach your target you will be ready to celebrate. Make sure that you do it publicly, using the press to spread news of your success. Make sure, too, that all those who have helped along the way, by giving their time or making donations, are thanked as far as you can. These people could be long-term supporters who will give much more over time if you nurture them and keep them up-to-date with your project's progress. Now is the time to consolidate your database. If you haven't already done so, log all the steps you took along the way, noting what worked and what didn't – ready for the next time. Your experience will be in demand after the event!

If you have a major project for funding and if you can muster the various skills and energy required, launching an appeal could be the best way to reach your fundraising target. It is enormously satisfying to run a major appeal successfully.

Case study

The success of the Hardton Children's Hospice Appeal was a blow to all the other charities in the town. It seemed that everyone was talking about the need to raise funds to build the new hospice – and nothing else. The local papers were full of it, the local radio station plugged it all the time – even conversation in the town's pubs and clubs revolved around it.

As Christmas approached, the local people were buying their cards to support the appeal, school and church fetes and fairs were raising money for the appeal, and anyone who was anyone had tickets to the gala performance of *Aladdin*, which was in aid of the appeal.

When asked in a newspaper interview for the secret of her success, Sandra Winner, chairperson of the appeal commented, 'It's not my success – it's the achievement of our extremely hardworking and dedicated committee who won't rest until everyone in this town has been touched by our appeal and done their bit for it. They have left no stone unturned.'

Of course, the basic principles that apply to running a major appeal apply equally to appeals on a smaller scale. Although the need for 'spot on' administrative skills and the ability to handle the press may not be so important, you can use the sections above for choosing a focus, planning, publicity, running the campaign and reaching your target. You may even be able to secure a 'big gift' to kick start your appeal.

Running an appeal through the press

Sometimes it is possible and appropriate to run an appeal through the press, either in an 'editorial' agreed with a newspaper, magazine, radio or television station (in which case the coverage will be free) or through paid advertisements. Previous experience of working with the media is valuable, though not essential provided that you are not intimidated by the media machine, and that you apply common sense to your planning and implementation.

Much of the planning and background work for an appeal run through the press will be similar to that of any other major appeal (see above). Once you have decided on the focus for your campaign, the critical element is to find the best medium for your message. Choose the radio station or magazine or newspaper that has an appropriate audience – one that will be sympathetic to your cause. There would be little point in trying to set up an appeal for a new church organ with a local radio station that plays mostly pop music and is listened to by an audience containing few church-goers. Fortunately, the programme makers and editors will help you here – they won't be interested if your appeal doesn't fit.

The benefit of running an appeal through the press is that once the message to be broadcast or published has been agreed, the production of the programme or printed material is in the hands of the professional producers and editors. It is vital, however, that you check details and make sure that the dates of broadcast or publication are relevant and that there is a clear response mechanism – listeners, viewers and readers must know where to send their donations. It is also critical that you are prepared to handle the response with enough staff or volunteers to process a mass of donations.

Provided that you are well-organized, have a strong focus for your campaign and can cope with the media, running an appeal through the press could be a useful fundraising technique for you.

The key steps to follow are:

■ choosing the focus for your campaign
■ selecting the right newspaper, magazine or pro-gramme for your message
■ planning the detail of your campaign with your media partner
■ setting up systems to handle donations
■ setting up a database of new supporters generated by the campaign.

On the subject of media appeals, it is possible to apply for funds from the major television appeals run by other organizations such as Comic Relief. You will need application forms supplied by their offices (see the Appendix for the address).

Fundraising events

Running a fundraising event, such as a ball or a banquet, a coffee morning or a car boot sale, may be an element of a major appeal or you may use this technique successfully in isolation. For a big event with high ticket prices you will need a defined and emotive cause, but it is still possible to cover the routine running costs of small organizations through fetes and fairs, sponsored walks and swims.

You won't need the level of expertise required to run a major appeal, but even a simple event requires some organizational ability and a major fundraiser, such as an open-air concert or a sponsored bike ride, will demand a high level of administrative skill and promotional flair. As many of these events are run on an annual basis, it is well worth documenting all the steps you take so that you establish a system for following years – especially if someone else will be at the helm next time around!

Besides fundraising, there are other significant benefits to be gained from running an event. Pulling a group together to run an event can be a great team-building exercise. While some of your

Good organization is the key to a successful event.

participants will be existing supporters, you should be able to attract new donors and volunteers. And a major function, especially if supported by celebrities or public figures, will attract publicity for your cause. You can build any of these as objectives into the plan for your event.

Types of event

Here are a few commonly used events that you could mould to your own purposes:

- auctions of promises
- bob-a-job
- quiz nights
- coffee mornings
- dinner dances
- balls and banquets
- bazaars and jamborees
- film and show premières
- concerts
- sponsored swims, runs, rides ets.
- fetes
- fairs and markets.

The list, of course, is endless and the more creative you are, the more you will be able to extend it. Creativity is vital, both in coming up with a new and motivating idea and in theming and presenting your event to appeal to your target audience. While it may be tempting to 'do the same thing as last year', donor fatigue is a real problem and innovation will be rewarded. The most important thing is to identify your potential audience first and then to create an event that will appeal to those people.

Ways of generating income

If you are running a concert or a film première, ticket sales will be the most obvious source of income. But don't overlook the possibility of getting sponsorship to cover your costs so that ticket income is pure profit. You should also be able to sell advertising space in your programme to businesses, and, of course, you can run 'events within events' for example, raffles and auctions at balls and banquets.

Sponsorship generated by individuals at fun runs and rides is a lower cost option (although it may take a good deal of manpower to man this sort of event safely, and you may need permission from the police, landowners or the local authority). Don't forget to sell any merchandise you may have – T-shirts and sweat-shirts, caps and pens – at the finishing line. At fetes and fairs, income will come from the stalls you run, or participation in fun and games!

Skills and resources

The level of skill you require will be commensurate with the scale of event you choose. There are pitfalls if you are over-ambitious or don't plan well enough. You may go to an enormous amount of effort and expense for a very small or even negative return. You should aim to raise at least £5 for every £1 spent. Bear in mind that many events run the risk of cancellation due to factors completely beyond the organizer's control. Insurance may be necessary. Events that involve a major capital outlay (such as balls and banquets where there are up-front costs for the hire of the venue, catering etc.) require not only intricate planning but also a major sales and promotion exercise to make sure that those costs are covered. Consider all of this as you decide if an event will meet your needs and if you have the skills and resources to run it.

Top of the list of skills and resources required for any event will be planning and organization. If you hope to find sponsorship, then business skills may be necessary. If you want to sell tickets, you must have energy, dedication and above all contacts. You will need promotional skills to make sure that your event achieves maximum exposure to your target audiences. Most importantly, you will need an army of willing supporters to provide all the necessary manpower.

With any event the key steps to follow are:

- targeting your audience
- choosing an appropriate event
- theming the event
- planning the details of the event and securing permission if relevant
- advertising and promotion
- finding sponsorship and selling tickets if applicable
- running the event
- gathering income, especially from sponsorship
- logging new supporters on your database.

Collections and lotteries

The good thing about these time-honoured techniques is that they can be used to cover core costs. Provided that your cause is worthy you do not necessarily need an exciting and motivating focal project. You will not need specialist skills nor a large fundraising budget – instead your success will depend on you finding plenty of willing, able and motivated manpower.

There are laws which govern these forms of fundraising, by which you must abide. You will probably need a permit from your local authority, and possibly permission from the police and private individuals or institutions, depending on where and how you wish to collect. One very important legal aspect is that collectors must be aged 16 or above. Children should not be left to knock on the doors of strangers.

Operating within the law

There are several Acts of Parliament which govern the conduct of house-to-house and street collections and lotteries (such as publicly promoted raffles and games of chance), and local authorities may use different procedures to ensure compliance. The licensing office of your local authority will send you application forms for permits, and will check your credentials as well as controlling a 'diary' of collections to avoid competing collections on the same day and in the same place. You will need to send an audited account of the proceeds of your collection or lottery to the licensing office.

When is a permit needed for a raffle or lottery?

There is a great deal of confusion about the need to apply for registration under the Lotteries and Amusements Act of 1976. You will need to pay £35 to your local authority for an annual registration (which is then renewable for an annual fee of £17.50) if you propose to run a 'public' lottery, raffle or game of chance where tickets are sold to the public in advance and separately from the draw or game itself. Where the value of the tickets will exceed £20,000 it will be necessary to register with the Gaming Board (contact details in the Appendix).

A lottery or raffle is considered private if the ticket sales and draw all take place at one event, e.g. a church fete or a school fair (even if this is open to the public), and in this case there is no requirement to be registered and no need for a permit. No more than £250 can be spent on buying prizes, and no cash prizes are allowed. Consult your local authority for further advice.

Planning

Planning is just as important with lotteries and collections as with any other form of fundraising – especially if a permit is required. The local authority issuing the permit will need to know when and where you wish to collect, how many collectors will be involved and whether any of these will be paid out of the proceeds of the collection – so you must think all this through well in advance.

Allow plenty of time – months rather than weeks – for the permit application, especially for a house-to-house collection. By law you are required to give your local authority a minimum of 28 days' notice. Where the authority also has to seek permission from relevant parish councils, the process can take considerably longer. Recruiting and briefing volunteers, sourcing collection boxes, setting up systems to handle incoming funds, and your own administration are all time-consuming tasks.

For your own success you need to choose carefully which streets are likely to yield the highest donations to your cause if you are collecting house-to-house, or which places – street corners, pubs, shopping malls etc. – will be most productive for collecting from passers-by. Don't forget to ask permission – pubs and shopping malls are privately owned! You will also need to consider what promotional material will best support and draw attention to your cause.

Recruiting and briefing volunteers

It is a common mistake to be so concerned with finding enough collectors that they go out onto the streets without being told clearly what to do. This type of collection involves a personal contact and so there is an opportunity to explain your cause as well as to fundraise for it. Your collectors should, at the very least, be able to explain your mission statement to any interested party, and may be able to do a great deal more to promote your cause if properly briefed.

Key tasks for those who are planning collections are:
- targeting appropriate areas and locations
- ensuring necessary permission is granted
- producing promotional materials, collection boxes etc.
- recruiting and briefing collectors
- gathering and paying in all income.

Case study

Delia Green could not understand why the collection she had organized for Barker's Dogs Home had been so poorly supported – and why the lady from the Council had been so cross with her. The collectors were all friends of hers – highly respectable ladies – and they had done their work on a Saturday morning so as not to be knocking on doors after dark. Most of the houses they had called on were within earshot of the home – so surely the people who lived there would be happy to give to such a local cause!

Mrs Kindly at the council office was losing her patience. She explained to Delia her catalogue of errors and hoped that it would all sink in! Delia had not applied for a permit from the council and so Mrs Kindly had been unable to tell Delia of another collection being taken in the same streets on the same day. While all Delia's volunteers were very nice ladies they carried no identification or note of authority from the Dogs Home to prove that they were bona fide collectors. Mrs Kindly also ventured to comment that people living closest to the home might not be its greatest supporters.

When Delia thought about it all, she could see that Mrs Kindly was only trying to be helpful and do her job. Next year Delia would apply for a permit in plenty of time and get a letter from the Dogs Home to endorse the collection – but she still didn't see why the local residents would not be supportive. 'Never mind', she thought to herself as she turned up her hearing aid to listen to the story on the wireless.

Direct mail

Although more criticized than any other fundraising technique, direct mail – the process of appealing for donations by post – can be highly effective when used correctly, and is worthy of consideration by most fundraising organizations, large and small. On a national scale, direct mail is highly sophisticated and generates huge sums of money. Large charities have their own direct mail departments or use specialist agencies, but the technique can also be used quite simply on a local level. The most important requirement is an accurate and appropriate mailing list. If you don't already have this you will have to invest time and money in building one. Once established, provided that it is kept up to date, a mailing list can be an extremely lucrative asset both for your own direct mail campaigns and for joint activities with other organizations or companies.

The more sophisticated your mailing efforts, the greater the need for direct marketing expertise. At a local level you should be able to run a successful campaign by post without specialist skills. You will have to invest time and money in creating and delivering your 'mail shot'. There will, inevitably, be wastage and your greatest challenge will be to keep this to a minimum. The key things to get right are the targeting of recipients, the 'mail piece' itself – especially the response mechanism – and the timing of your campaign.

Targeting

Quite simply, if you ask people who are sympathetic to your cause you are more likely to get a positive response. You will need to apply a good deal of common sense to identifying those who are most likely to support you, and you will need sound administrative skills to build an accurate and up-to-date mailing list of those prospects. Record the names and addresses of anyone who shows any interest in your organization – people who give to you, of course, but also those who ask you for information or who supply you with goods or services. Build up a list of everyone with whom you have contact, checking that you may mail them further information.

The mail piece

Although yours may be a very worthy cause, the piece of paper that you send to potential donors may be classed as 'junk mail' along with all the other unsolicited mail that most households receive. The more relevant and appealing it is to the recipient, the better the chance that it will, at least, be read. Choose a project or theme for your mail shot that will motivate your target audience. Make sure that it contains a clear central message that seeks a direct response. You will need a combination of creative flair and common sense to make sure that the message you send touches your targeted audience and achieves a response. Whatever the message and however you present it, you should include a response mechanism such as a coupon or a pre-paid reply envelope to capitalize on the interest your mail piece generates.

Responses and timing

As with all other fundraising techniques that are likely to attract a sudden influx of funds, you should have systems in place to cope with the extra donations. Response rates will vary enormously, of course. You may get little or nothing from a 'cold' mailing to people with whom you have had no previous connection. You may get an enormous response if you mail existing supporters with a particularly poignant appeal. Some supporters are very comfortable with the catalogue and mail culture and will give more readily in response to a direct mail shot, while others may find it off-putting. You can make use of your lists to do further mailings, but you will need to exercise good judgement to avoid asking for too much or too often.

Timing will depend very much on your own circumstances, but do make sure you allow plenty of time for people to respond and, if you can, avoid the pre-Christmas rush when every other charity will be mailing your prospects too!

Direct mail can be useful to small organizations as a one-off campaign to raise funds for a particular project or appeal, but it also has a value when lists are developed and used a number of times over a period of years. While it is unlikely to be your sole means of fundraising, direct mail can be an effective component of the overall fundraising mix.

Key tasks for direct mailers include:

- building a mailing list
- identifying a motivating focal project or theme
- putting together the mail piece
- timing your mail shot
- handling responses
- updating your database.

Fundraising from grant-making bodies

In this section we will cover fundraising from statutory bodies, trusts, foundations and also from the lottery boards as the techniques used are very similar. Almost every charity should be able to have a go at fundraising from grant-making bodies appropriate to its cause. A commitment to research and the ability to write a persuasive proposal will certainly help your chances of success, and in some cases effective lobbying can make a difference. There is no doubt that practice makes perfect and that the more experience you have of this area the greater you may expect the rewards to be.

Dedication to the task is essential. You are unlikely to find money quickly in an emergency by approaching a grant-making body –

although there will always be exceptions. Such bodies are more likely to yield long-term and repeatable donations that offer valuable support to small organizations. In a few rare cases the grants may be non-project specific and, where this is the case, can be used to cover core costs or finance an otherwise unattractive project. However, the application procedures can be tortuous, and, because the grants are often dispensed by a committee that may meet only once a quarter, the time frames can be painfully long.

Research

Thorough, systematic research is the key to successful fundraising from grant-making bodies. Because they exist to give, most trusts, foundations, and certainly the lottery boards are inundated with appeals for funds on a daily basis. Some of these appeals will not even fall within the remit of that funding body. Finding a grant-making trust that actively supports the sort of work you do can be a time-consuming desk job, but it is essential if your application for funds is to stand any chance of success.

There are a number of invaluable guides, in particular *The Directory of Grant Making Trusts* and *A Guide to the Major Trusts*, published by the Directory of Social Change (see address in the Appendix) that are available to buy or can be found in libraries. These will help you to identify trusts that will be sympathetic to your cause. They also contain information on the size of grants made and geographical bias.

Fortunately, desk research is low cost and can be carried out by a single dedicated volunteer. There are computer-driven packages such as Grant Seeker (available from DSC) and FunderFinder (address in the Appendix) to help you identify potential supporters, if you can justify the cost.

Networking and lobbying

There is no doubt that who you know can influence your chances of success in this area. If you intend to major on fundraising from statutory bodies, it can be very helpful to get to know not only the system, but also the people who operate within it. 'Lobbying' is commonplace in all sorts of government circles.

Finding a grant–making trust can be time-consuming.

Making an application

Many grant-making bodies have specific application procedures
and forms. These may leave little room for creativity and demand
attention to detail instead. Whether you use an application form or
simply apply for a grant by letter, it is vital that your appeal is clear,
concise, motivating and relevant to that particular grant-making
body – so you will need good writing skills. Do include your
mission statement and perhaps an annual report if these documents
supplement and do not duplicate the contents of your letter. If your
research has identified a telephone number for your targeted trust,
don't be afraid to ring and ask how your application is progressing.
You could offer further information if applicable, but don't pester
busy secretaries of grant-making bodies to the point where you put
them off.

Following up

It may take some time for a response to come through, or there may
be no response at all. If you are lucky you will receive a grant, in
which case it is vital that it is acknowledged and that the donor is

kept informed of your project's progress. Building a rapport with the trustees may lead to further grants and these will be far more cost-effective than sourcing new ones.

If your application is rejected, do ask the reason why and whether it would be worth applying again for a grant for a different project, or at a different time. Some trusts try to discourage this sort of contact, usually because they are very busy, but it can only help to develop a better understanding between grant seekers and grant makers – this has to be advantageous to all concerned.

Key tasks to secure donations include:

- research
- making a written application for funds
- following up by phone
- thanking donors and building on their support.

Corporate fundraising

There are a number of different techniques to be covered here, held together by the fact that they all solicit money from companies. As we discussed in the last chapter on sources of funding, companies give money from two key areas – the 'charitable' budget and the more commercial marketing or PR budget. Different techniques are required to access each.

Corporate income is a valuable addition to any organization's coffers. Substantial sums can be generated, but donations will almost certainly be linked to very specific projects from which the company will expect major benefits. Usually the greater the sum, the greater the effort the charity will have to make for it – you get what you work for!

Companies can be very useful partners in other ways. They have skills, facilities and equipment that you may be able to access. They have a pool of staff who might be prepared to fundraise for you. And they can open doors to other organizations on your behalf. Most organizations would benefit from developing one or two commercial partnerships provided that the match between company and charity is right.

Accessing funds locally and nationally

At a local level you may still find individuals within companies who can give small sums for charitable purposes without looking for much in return – and it is well worth finding and tapping these. Try especially the managers of local branches of major banks, building societies and supermarkets. Use personal contacts and local knowledge to identify potential supporters.

But mostly, and certainly on a national scale, you will have to put forward good reasons as to why a company should support you. The deeper your understanding of the factors that motivate companies to give, the stronger your proposals to them will be – and the greater your chances of success. In every approach you should put great emphasis on identifying the benefits to your potential partner.

Asking for money from charitable budgets

The first and most important thing is to target the right company – one that has a budget available to support the sort of work you wish to fund. You will have to apply yourself to desk research, supplemented by personal knowledge, to identify suitable potential donors and determine how they wish to be approached for funds.

Creating a carefully tailored proposal that meets the needs of the corporate donor, presenting it personally if you are given the opportunity, being open to discussion and negotiation, and following it through vigorously, are the key elements of the fundraising process.

Delving into marketing and PR budgets

There is much greater scope here, both in terms of the sums available and the ways in which you can tap them, but there is also greater danger, because you will be entering a partnership and you must be absolutely certain that you can deliver your part of the joint activity. Legally binding contracts will apply and for this reason your trustees, who have legal responsibility for the management of your organization, should be fully involved in any decision to seek funds in this way.

Sponsorship

At the simpler end of this more commercial fundraising is the time-honoured sponsorship of a particular project or event. Many small organizations are very successful in securing corporate income of this kind. Corporate sponsorship can be most valuable for covering the costs of a fundraising event so that all of the proceeds go straight to the project. Finding a sponsor who is motivated by the type of event, or its theme, or the project which the funds will benefit, is important. Finding a sponsor who needs the public awareness, or entertainment opportunities, or other commercial benefit that your event offers, is the key.

Joint promotions

Joint charity/company promotional activity is an exciting area, but not one for the faint-hearted. Here a company will expect a measurable increase in corporate or brand awareness, if not a direct increase in sales, in exchange for its donation. There are a million ways to collaborate like this with a company, but classic examples are the on-pack promotions found on every supermarket shelf.

Case study

A major cancer research charity joined forces with a well-known brand of bran-based breakfast cereal in a joint promotion worth £1 million. The money was pledged to help raise public awareness about how bowel cancer could be prevented – an issue of supreme relevance for both parties.

The promotion was flagged on every packet of the cereal, giving the charity additional publicity for its cause. The literature that explained the links between diet and bowel cancer carried the cereal's branding. All in all this was a mutually beneficial exercise, but one carried out with the highest levels of professionalism and a major investment of time on both sides.

Licensing

Licensing is the other option for fundraising from companies. Here a royalty will be paid for every product sold that carries the charity's name, logo or branding. This will be of most use to you if you have an extremely well-known or covetable name or brand or logo, and so is most often used by the big, high-profile charities. Getting the product/charity match right is vital. There can be serious pitfalls if you choose an inappropriate partner – public outcry and loss of support may result.

Case study

There was enormous upset when the name of the late Diana, Princess of Wales, was used to generate royalties for her charity through a licensing deal with a brand of margarine. The promotion was considered to be inappropriate by many and generated bad publicity.

It may be possible to use a licensing mechanism on a smaller scale with, for example, a local restaurant donating a percentage from the price of a particular dish. One of the major pizza chains supported the Venice in Peril campaign by giving a sum for each Venezia pizza sold.

Approaching companies – how to do it

Identifying an appropriate company comes first and foremost, trying to find a potential partner that will fit neatly with your own organization. Once you have a target in mind try to work out what that company needs in terms of marketing and PR, and how a link with your organization could meet some of those needs. From this you will be able to produce a list of benefits to the company that would come from a partnership with you. Draft a document for discussion that identifies ways in which you could work together and the benefits of doing so.

Find the person within the company who is best placed to reach a deal with you, and post, fax or e-mail your document for his or her attention. Follow the document up with a phone call to secure, if you can, a meeting. Once you have a foot inside the door you are well on your way, but don't expect your plans to stay fixed – be ready to discuss, accommodate and negotiate.

Corporate fundraising – the necessary skills

Tapping corporate budgets, whether charitable or commercial, is a specialist skill and one that requires patience and dedication. The corporate decision-making process can be slow and frustrating. It will usually take months to research, present, negotiate and secure a corporate deal.

With corporate fundraising in particular, 'knowledge is everything'. Who you know and what you know will have a major impact on your fundraising achievements. For this reason it certainly helps to have worked in the business world, to speak the language of business and preferably to command business skills. 'Networking' or getting to know people in the corporate world will help to open doors that otherwise might remain obstinately shut.

Any organization thinking of trying companies for funding should consider whether it is appropriate. Corporate fundraising demands a substantial input in terms of skilled manpower – to do the asking in the first place but, just as importantly, to 'service' any resulting corporate partnership. As you may be entering the realms of a legally binding contract it is vital that the company gets everything it has been promised in return for its donation. The more complex the fundraising technique, the greater the effort the charity will have to make. Many small organizations are caught unawares and are overwhelmed.

Having said that, if you choose your target companies and methods of approach carefully, if you take your time and you are not too ambitious on your first attempts, this can be a rewarding and lucrative area.

Key tasks for corporate fundraisers are:

- researching and targeting potential corporate donors
- producing proposals with benefits to the donor
- securing meetings to discuss proposals
- presenting ideas
- negotiating a deal

- agreeing a contract
- implementing the agreement and building relationships.

Community fundraising and individual endeavour

If you are very short of resources or don't have the skills to manage some of the other fundraising techniques discussed so far, you may find that others will be prepared to fundraise for you. While it would be unwise to rely entirely on the efforts of individuals or groups in your local community, their contributions can play a major part in your fundraising plan. You may find that you have a gift for motivating others to do all sorts of weird and wonderful things on your behalf – many a parachute or bungee jump has been made by an individual determined to do his or her bit for a local charity.

Even if you have other fundraising projects underway and are heavily involved in a capital appeal, a major event or corporate fundraising, tapping the efforts of others on your behalf can be a useful way of spreading your sources of income so that you do not become too dependent on any one.

There are, however, pitfalls for the unwary here. Most common is the unsolicited approach from an individual, maybe a student, who wishes to undertake some sort of expedition, climb or trek ostensibly on your behalf and ostensibly to raise money for you. While often these are genuine intentions, the driving force for the activity may be simply the individual's desire to raft down the Zambezi or conquer a Himalayan peak. Sometimes the charity is a necessary vehicle without which the rafter or climber would never raise the funds to get to his or her start point. The important thing is to sift the good fundraising prospects from the ones that are more likely to cost you money – and possibly time and reputation as well.

Make sure that your benefactor can complete the activity without excessive input from you – and that he or she doesn't bring your cause into disrepute! It may be simpler to reject some offers of this kind than to become ensnared in someone else's problems.

Case study

An international relief agency was approached by a young man who wished to raise money for it by cycling an ancient trading route across the Far and Middle East. The agency agreed but, as it was heavily involved in other projects, left much of the detail and organization to the young man. He attracted a good deal of publicity and some sponsorship but, unfortunately, had not acquired all the necessary travel documents and was detained by the authorities at his third border crossing.

Because he was travelling under the banner of the agency it became heavily involved in securing his release – a time-consuming task. The resulting delays meant he was unable to complete the journey so that sponsorship was not realized and the publicity turned sour.

Sources of community support

There are, however, plenty of bona fide groups within the community who you could approach, or who might volunteer to fundraise for you, or to support you in some other way. The most obvious are associations such as the Round Table, Lions, Rotary Clubs, Soroptomists groups, Chambers of Commerce, Young Farmers, Townswomen's Guilds and Women's Institutes. Some of these will be happy to fundraise for you through their own events – others may offer volunteers to help you run your own projects. Some will be invaluable as a means of networking within your community or promoting your cause by speaking at their gatherings.

Other groups, as diverse as your local branch of the Scouts or the customers from your local pub, may well be willing to run anything from sponsored car washes to fundraising quiz nights on your behalf. The better known your organization is within the local community, the more your community will give back.

Key tasks for raising funds with community support include:

- choosing reliable partners
- agreeing and planning activities

- collecting funds raised
- building relationships for future fundraising.

Tax-effective giving

Whichever technique you choose to raise funds, it makes sense to enhance the value of donations wherever possible. Tax-effective giving can increase the value of a gift because the charity can reclaim tax at the basic rate paid by the donor on his or her income. Wherever you can, encourage your donors to give by Deed of Covenant if the support is likely to be long-term, or by Gift Aid for a larger one-off donation.

Small charities can also benefit from tax-effective payroll giving such as the Give As You Earn scheme run by CAF. Under these schemes any individual can choose to support any bona fide charity, but concerted campaigns to promote a cause to targeted employees are normally the province of the large, well-staffed charities!

Other fundraising techniques

There are, of course, many other ways of raising funds that have not been covered in depth here because they are less relevant to smaller organizations.

Telephone appeals, for example, demand considerable manpower and are expensive to run. As with direct mail they depend heavily on good lists of potential supporters and on the persuasive powers of the caller. For this reason they have had a bad press and many potential supporters may be put off by the perceived intrusion of the calls into their private time and homes. The Institute of Charity Fundraising Managers (ICFM – contact details in the Appendix) has a code of practice for telephone fundraising.

The ICFM and the Charity Commission both discourage the use of **chain letters** as a means of fundraising. While chain letters are cheap and easy to set up they are almost impossible to control. Your charity could be open to claims of misleading the public if your appeal target has been met but a chain letter requesting funds for the appeal continues to run away with itself.

Some small organizations are run on a **membership** basis and it is perfectly acceptable in some cases to charge a fee and thereby raise funds. This sort of operation frequently goes with a more complex structure that offers membership benefits and possibly voting rights.

Trading in any item, from a simple badge to a catalogue full of Christmas goodies, can be a useful fundraising technique, but economies of scale generally make it more useful for larger organizations that can afford to invest in stock. Having said that, every PTA can produce a calendar for sale at the school gates, possibly with the costs of production covered by a local corporate sponsor. Other simple items that you could produce yourself might include tea towels and Christmas cards. Diaries, pens, mugs and T shirts can be bought in and overprinted with your own message, name or logo.

While many small organizations, especially those with an older base of supporters, benefit by good fortune from **legacies**, it is mainly the major national charities that can cover the expense of an effective legacy campaign. By its very nature, raising funds through legacies requires an investment of time and money that may not be recovered for years.

If you do decide to plan a formal legacy fundraising campaign, try working with a local solicitor who can advise you on current legal issues and may be able to help you with promotion. Knowledge of your own supporters through personal contact and use of your database are also, of course, extremely important in terms of targeting appropriate benefactors. Promoting a legacy campaign to others who don't already support you can be a very expensive business, and, again, the aggressive 'selling' of legacy campaigns by some of the larger charities has generated negative comment about legacy fundraising – so be prepared.

Obviously you will need tact and diplomacy to turn a supporter into a legacy donor. You will also need an extremely good administrator to keep track of any legacies you are able to generate, and to follow through the process of securing the legacy once the donor has died. Bear in mind that wills can be contested.

If you don't have the resources to handle all these issues effectively, it may be best simply to be grateful for the legacies that do come your way.

Questions and answers

Selecting the right fundraising techniques

Q *There are so many different ways of raising money. How do I start to choose the right ones?*

A Take stock of what you need to achieve, in terms of income, and the resources (the time, money, skills and experience) you have available. Then match the fundraising methods to suit.

If you need to raise a small amount of money and don't have a great deal of fundraising experience keep your fundraising methods simple to start with. Try the time-honoured raffles, collections and simple fundraising events. As you become more confident and more experienced you may wish to try something more ambitious.

Don't tackle the more complex events, major appeals or corporate fundraising techniques unless you have the skills to follow them through.

Choosing a name for an appeal

Q *How important is a catchy name for an appeal?*

A Everything you can do to promote your appeal to the relevant audience is important. If you are about to choose a name then, of course, go for something that will fix itself in the minds of your potential donors. Make sure that the name reflects the values of your organization, and draw up a promotional plan to ensure maximum exposure of your appeal to those likely to support it.

Inviting royalty to open or attend events

Q *My charity is only small but we are based near the home of a minor member of the royal family. We would like her to be our guest of honour at our annual fundraising ball. Should we give it a try?*

A Do bear in mind that the royal family is in great demand and if there is no specific link with your organization you may not be considered. Having royalty present does also raise security issues so be certain that you can cope with those. If you wish to go ahead you should make a simple request in writing months in advance because royal diaries are committed so far ahead.

If your request is not successful, or if you decide that a different approach might be better anyway, try a local dignitary or celebrity. You may find that he or she could give more time to your charity and become more involved in your work than could a member of the royal family. An active celebrity patron might be of much greater value than a single visit from royalty.

Trying new fundraising techniques

Q *Our PTA committee is divided over how to raise funds for some new equipment for the gym. I think we should stick to the tried and tested methods of Christmas fairs and summer fetes, raffles and coffee mornings. One new PTA member says she has contacts with a computer firm and she wants to approach them for a donation. What do you think?*

A Don't be afraid to try new methods of fundraising as long as they are appropriate to your situation and you have the skills required to carry them through. It is good to diversify and not to rely too heavily on one type of income.

It would be a pity to waste your new colleague's enthusiasm, especially if she has relevant contacts. Try to establish if she also has any business acumen – it could be a great asset to you.

If your colleague simply wants to seek a charitable donation from the computer firm, you have little or nothing to lose. In the unlikely event that she is thinking of some all singing, all dancing commercial partnership where the company would expect some benefit in return for its donation, you may have to be a little more cautious. Suggest that your colleague takes advice from the corporate fundraising sections of this book before approaching the company.

Preventing misrepresentation by others

Q *It worries me when another organization, be it the local school or village pub, offers to fundraise on my charity's behalf. I am afraid that they might, inadvertently, misrepresent our organization. What can I do to prevent this?*

A You are right to protect your charity's name and all it represents as far as you can, but don't become a control freak – you may miss out on valuable support.

When another organization offers to fundraise for you meet those involved to discuss their plans and to make sure they are appropriate. Take time to present your charity to them so that they are fully aware of your ethos and the image you try to project. They want to help you, so the closer their understanding of your charity the better. Prepare a simple sheet that shows how your name and logo should be used and ask to see drafts of their materials if you are still concerned. If you develop a close understanding and a good working relationship with each other, you may benefit from a valuable long-term partnership.

This advice applies whoever the partner may be. A company will expect a more formal exchange of views, especially if there is a contractual obligation, but, again, the more trust and mutual understanding the better.

9 | ESSENTIAL SKILLS AND FINDING FURTHER ADVICE

So there you are! You have prepared meticulously, setting your house in order and paving the way for your fundraising approaches. You know where your target income might come from and which methods are most appropriate to help you secure it. You are ready to devise your fundraising strategy. Once it is in place, all that is left is to go out and implement it.

This sounds simple, but of course it helps if you know how to write an effective proposal, how to tackle a presentation, how to negotiate a better deal and how to build relationships. Practice makes perfect, but this chapter will guide you as you acquire those essential skills.

Writing a 'proposal'

The first thing to consider here is whether you should be producing a 'proposal' for funding at all, or whether it would be better to prepare a 'discussion document'. If you are approaching a grant-making body, such as a trust or a health authority, you will, almost certainly, need to put forward concrete proposals, the key elements of which we will cover later.

Far too many charities rush headlong into creating the same watertight proposal that includes all the vital elements of costs and benefits, project summary and timeframe, for all potential donors – regardless of who they are. Everything is set and in its place, leaving no room for discussion or negotiation. Furthermore, because everything has been worked out so precisely, there is no opportunity to accommodate the views of the potential donor.

The secret is to think of your potential donor as a partner, and the 'discussion document' you produce to introduce your project should offer to discuss your partner's views, needs and ideas so that they can be incorporated, where appropriate, into your joint venture. If you can be flexible you will open many doors. It may take a shift of your organizational mind-set to think of donors as partners, but it will definitely be worthwhile.

Case study

A small charity approached a local company with a proposal for the company to fund the production of its annual report. The correspondence was in writing and the fundraiser was terrified when the managing director requested a meeting. Face to face the fundraiser presented his case and was delighted when the managing director agreed to fund the report.

Flush with success, the fundraiser decided to mention other promotional literature for which funding was required urgently. In a long discussion over lunch they discussed the benefits of working together – the managing director was only too pleased to have his company's logo on all the charity's literature and agreed to fund the lot.

This fundraiser was lucky because he plucked up the courage to discuss other needs. He could have made his prospects stronger from the start by offering to discuss a range of projects with the company.

Key elements of a proposal

Apart from that vital element of **flexibility** and the **offer to discuss** suggested projects in more detail, the key elements of any 'proposal' are the **project summary** which outlines what you hope to achieve, including the benefits to the charity. Donors like to know that their contribution has made a difference. Next are the perceived **benefits to the donor** – think of all the possible advantages to your targeted donor of supporting the project. You may well find that others emerge in discussion and negotiation. Your **timeframe** may be set, in which case make it clear, but you may have to negotiate over **costs**. Make sure that you have a figure in mind below which you cannot go, and a figure on paper that will achieve your aims in more comfort, for discussion if necessary. You will find a sample of a 'proposal' or 'discussion document' at the end of Chapter 10.

Of course your proposal should be carefully targeted at a specific donor with features that you believe will be interesting and relevant to him or her. Blanket mailings of bland proposals are not worth the paper they are written on. Any proposal that you have mailed should be followed up with a phone call a few days later to suggest a meeting to discuss your project in detail. If you achieve this then your proposal has done its job.

Presenting

Fundraising is one thing, but standing up in front of a room full of people to sing the praises of your project is quite another! You may well have to do this to persuade others to give you their support. It's all about confidence, of course, and that will come with practice, but it also comes from being well prepared.

Formal presentations

As with most other things in life, good planning is the key. Every presentation should be made with a clear aim or objective in mind. It may be to secure a deal or it could be just to move to further discussion. Work out the message you need to get across to your audience to achieve your aim – it should probably contain three or four key points. If you are pitching for funding, for example, you will want to describe your project, explain the need for funding, and set out the benefits of being associated with your project. You may wish to lay out your credentials or present testimonials at the end.

Divide your presentation into clear sections, each of which will cover one of your key points. You may wish to illustrate what you are saying with videos, slides, overheads or computer-driven visuals. Make sure that they, and what you say, are brief, informative and relevant. Don't try to memorize a full speech – work from bullet points that will trigger what you need to say and help to keep you to the point.

Start your presentation with a welcome to your audience and an agenda of the points you wish to cover. Finish with an invitation to discuss. Be prepared for interruptions and discussion as you go along, but make sure that you are not diverted from saying what you need to say.

Always rehearse your presentation with an audience of colleagues, friends or family – or just the cat if you prefer. Make sure that you have run through it to check for length and that any props you propose to use such as slides, videos or overheads work correctly. On the day, try to install yourself and any equipment you need in plenty of time so that you are not worried about technical details when the presentation begins. Don't be too ambitious and do take a colleague for moral support if it makes you feel more confident.

Rehearse your presentation with an audience.

Ultimately your audience will be swayed more by your own conviction than by anything else, so don't allow any nerves to swamp your own commitment and dedication to your cause.

At the end you will probably have the opportunity to leave supporting material. Choose this carefully to make sure that it is relevant and of good quality. This is an occasion to use your mission statement, your case for support and possibly other material such as a brochure or annual report.

Informal presentations

The same ground rules apply to informal presentations of your work that take place over lunch or in a meeting with just a few other people. It is critical that you have worked out your overall aim or objective and the key points you need to cover. While you may not be able to deliver them in any set pattern, you must make sure that you get them all across. Produce an agenda for the meeting so that everyone knows what you want to discuss.

Formal props may not be appropriate but you may be able to introduce photos, charts or diagrams to add interest to what you are saying and to help you make your point. You should leave supporting material, just as you would in a more formal situation.

Making an effective presentation, whether formal or informal, is something of an art. The more you do the more you will develop a feel for how to steer a conversation to the crucial point and how to engage an audience in what you say.

Negotiating – asking for money

Many people find they have in-built inhibitions when it comes to asking for money. The simplest way to tackle this is to put your commitment to your cause up front. You must ask clearly and directly for what you want, but you will find it easier to do so if you don't lose sight of exactly what that money will achieve. Explain to your donor why the money is so important so that he or she 'buys in' to your proposition. Practice will make perfect.

Sometimes it is appropriate to attach a specific price tag to a project and to ask for that amount – a grant from a trust, for example, would be tackled like this. There are other occasions, particularly when dealing with companies, where you may have to negotiate.

Negotiation is a specialist skill and will take time and practice to perfect, but, essentially, you are aiming for each party to believe that they have benefited from the transaction – the classic 'win/win' situation. If you are so hard in your dealings that the donor feels beaten down, you are unlikely to win support. You, however, must not allow the donor to take unfair advantage. Using the good old bazaar technique of setting your price a little higher than necessary and being prepared to barter may make everyone feel they have a good deal at the end of the negotiation.

Growing support and building relationships

It is far easier to source money from an existing supporter than to find new ones, and for this reason every one of your donors should be valued and nurtured. Clear and honest communication is essential. With companies, trusts and foundations this will mean holding regular progress meetings or issuing progress reports. Site visits and invitations to social gatherings will help to build a relationship with your donor so that it is easier to ask for further funding when the time comes. Make sure that any publications such as annual reports or newsletters are sent to your major supporters. The closer their involvement with you the more difficult it will be for them to say 'no' the next time you need to ask.

Individual donors should be thanked wherever possible and be given the opportunity to become involved in other ways, as volunteers or possibly as committee members. Up-dating your database should be an ongoing task so that your list of supporters can be mobilized at any time.

Monitoring success

Every church organ appeal has its progress chart just inside the lytch gate. It serves to promote the cause and to inspire further action. Every fundraising campaign should be monitored in this way, not publicly necessarily, but certainly so that those who are fundraising can judge their achievements and see where greater effort is required.

Your financial systems will vary in complexity depending on the scale of your appeal, but you should be able to produce a financial status report on, at least, a monthly basis. It should give, where possible, a breakdown of different income sources so that you can assess the success or otherwise of various fundraising methods. It should show progress in relation to previous months so that weaker periods can be identified, and it should chart overall progress towards your target so that you can adjust your strategy to meet new challenges before they become crises. The financial status report should be a working document for all those involved in fundraising to help keep their efforts focused, as well as to inspire and motivate!

Further training and advice

Fortunately there are a number of highly professional organizations that specialize in furthering the aims of charities. Several, such as the Directory of Social Change, offer training for charity work and some have comprehensive lists of publications which will give you further advice on just about every aspect of fundraising. The Institute of Charity Fundraising Managers (ICFM) is the professional body for fundraisers. It sets codes of practice and professional standards and offers opportunities for further training. All addresses, phone numbers, websites and other contact details can be found in the Appendix.

Questions and answers

Presentation formats

Q *I always think that overheads look old fashioned, but our small charity can't afford computer generated visuals for formal presentations. What do you suggest we use?*

A There are plenty of different presentation formats to chose from, and you should use whatever is appropriate to your situation. If you are a small charity a computer driven presentation might look completely out of place. It might give the message that you are better off than you really are – so don't hanker for it!

The overall impression generated by your presentation and the key messages to come out of it are more important than the presentation format itself. So if you choose slides or overheads or a video be sure that you are comfortable using them and that the necessary equipment is in place and working properly before you start. A technical hitch will distract your audience and leave you feeling flustered. Simple, carefully prepared flip charts can be just as effective as more sophisticated formats.

Make sure that the format you use is appropriate for the space in which you have to present and the number of people in your audience. Be certain to tailor what you say to that audience and don't be tempted to run a standard presentation just because it's easier.

Remember it is the relevance of your message and the conviction with which you present it that count more than anything else.

Entertaining donors to build support

Q *I can't believe it is right for charities to 'entertain' donors. How can I build good relationships with our supporters without spending money on them?*

A You don't have to take your donors out to lunch! Many donors would be thrilled to visit projects at their own expense. So if you have a site around which they can be shown this could be the best move for you.

Try also to build rapport with your donors through progress reports and meetings. If you do run any social events invite your key donors, even if you ask them to pay for a ticket. Make sure that your donors are on your mailing list for any newsletters, annual reports or other promotional material that you produce. Good communication will count for a lot more than a trip to the pub!

Negotiating part funding of projects

Q *If my negotiation doesn't go quite according to plan, should I accept less for my project than it is worth?*

A You should be prepared for this possibility before you enter the negotiation. Not that you should be negative, just that you should have covered every eventuality. You will never be absolutely certain of what is in your donor's mind.

So you must consider, and agree with all relevant colleagues, whether part funding would be acceptable to you or not. If you believe your project is strong and that other donors might fund it in full, you might reject the possibility of part funding. If you think that your project could be split for funding purposes and that another donor might sponsor a different part of it you could accept. In this case you would probably reduce the benefit to each sponsor or find some way of sharing the benefit between the two.

For example, you might offer title sponsorship of your open air concert to your local car dealer so that it would be called 'Automan's Prom in the Park'– in aid of Paterbury Hospice. If Automan agreed only to part funding of the concert you might withdraw its name from the title but add 'sponsored by Automan' to all promotional activities. You should negotiate benefits in proportion to the funding offered.

You may simply feel that part funding is better than nothing and accept it without making any changes to the benefits the sponsor will receive, but beware of undermining your own position for the next time you try to negotiate.

10 THE FUNDRAISING STRATEGY

This is the culmination of everything that we have covered in this book. All the knowledge of systems and resources, products and promotion, sources of income and methods of tapping them that you have acquired can now be applied as you prepare your own unique fundraising strategy. At the end of the chapter you will find a sample fundraising strategy, promotional plan and proposal/discussion document to help you shape your own ideas.

Strategic planning

Strategic planning should not be simply a mechanical process. If your strategic thinking is not inspired and visionary, you will find it hard to implement your plan with true conviction. It is your passion for your cause and your dedication to it that will be the strongest influencing factors in all your dealings with potential donors. So, while the planning process must be logical and based upon what is realistic, the finished plan must also motivate and inspire.

Assessing the current situation

The strategic planning process should, of course, start by assessing your current situation. You need to know what your existing sources of income deliver and how much more is required. You need to know what resources are available to you in terms of budget, manpower, skills and equipment. And this is the point at which you can use the findings of your SWOT analysis to pinpoint key opportunities and to highlight particular areas of strength.

Everything you do as a fundraiser should dovetail with your organization's overall strategic plan for the next three to five years and should serve the needs it identifies. Everything should, of course, be consistent with your mission statement, so it is necessary to assess where your organization stands in relation to its overall objectives. From all of this you should be able to identify your priorities as a fundraiser.

Setting aims and objectives

What are those priorities? What do you want, or need, to achieve from your fundraising activities? You may have one simple overall aim to reach a specific financial target – perhaps to raise £10,000 for a new play structure for the local playground. You may also have a set of contributing objectives, such as to realize £5,000 of the total required from statutory sources, £3,000 from fundraising events and £2,000 from community contributions. You may also wish to secure a 'gift in kind' from the local private school to supply the services of its groundsman to maintain the new equipment.

Or you may have a long-term aim to bring in £50,000 from a range of sources within the next two years, but also a short-term objective to turn a budget deficit into an operating profit within three months. The important thing is that each of your aims and objectives should be clear, realistic and measurable – you, and others around you such as your trustees, staff, volunteers and supporters, will want to know when you have achieved them!

Take care to blend your vision with reality. The amount of time, commitment and expertise you can muster will be deciding factors in what you can achieve, but there will also be many factors outside your control – conflicting activities and competing demands on other people's budgets – that may impact on your fundraising.

Methods

How do you propose to meet your aims and objectives? Now you must apply some creative and strategic thinking to consider the range of different fundraising methods that could meet your requirements. Which of these will best suit your purposes? Bearing in mind your current levels of expertise and resources you might feel it is most appropriate to fundraise principally from individuals, in which case you might plan a street collection, a Christmas fair and an auction of promises. Or you may feel that you are ready to tackle the corporate sector, in which case you may choose to ask for money from charitable budgets or to try a licensing programme. The most effective strategies will combine a number of different techniques which tap income from a range of sources – you should aim for a broad base of support where possible.

The fundraising plan

As you select those methods most likely to meet your objectives you will be defining a programme of work that will be required. This will be the plan of campaign that you put into action to meet your fundraising targets.

You may find that you need to produce a plan for each type of fundraising activity – you might, for example, have a plan for a direct mail campaign and another for fundraising from trusts. Each plan should target a donor or set of donors very specifically and outline the activities that will be necessary to persuade them to give. You will, almost certainly, need to produce a complementary promotional or PR plan that will pave the way for, and support, your fundraising approaches. Each individual plan of activity should dovetail into the overall strategy that you have decided upon.

Timeframe

Every part of the plan should have a deadline by which it must be completed if you are to realize your goals. Make sure that it is realistic and that it takes into account the time that others will take to supply you with necessary resources, such as printed materials, and the time that your donors may take to respond to you.

Costs and resources

All fundraising carries a cost in either time or money and you must plan for this. You should consider whether you will need additional resources to carry out your plan – perhaps a brochure, or maybe more staff or volunteers. All of this should be carefully budgeted and compared with your fundraising target to make sure that you are spending in reasonable proportion to the income expected.

Review

Every good strategy should include a mechanism for reviewing progress and renewing the process of strategic planning when the time comes. Build in a system for weekly, monthly or possibly quarterly assessments of where you stand in relation to your targets. You may need to modify parts of your plan if some parts of it have proven unsuccessful.

Approval

You may work alone and you may not have to answer to anyone – but this is rare. Most fundraisers will require the approval of their trustees, senior management or fellow committee members, if not their active involvement, in the creation of a fundraising strategy. It is vital to ensure that your strategy has the necessary approval before you try to implement it!

Case study

Little Angels School playframe appeal was very fortunate to have a highly motivated and active fundraiser who saw no problem in raising the £6,000 required to add a much needed piece of equipment to the play area. Gloria Getter sat through committee meetings because she had to – what she loved was going out and swinging the deals.

Because she had read this book, Gloria knew that she had to plan her approach. Although some of it was a bit of a bore she targeted and researched her donors, made sure of the fundraising methods she wanted to use to reach the target, and even produced some costings and a timetable.

Unfortunately, in her excitement to get on with the job, she skipped the last few pages of the book and didn't read the section on approval. She rushed into action, setting up a sponsored swim, a promotion with the local paper and a deal with the nearby sports centre, all within the first two weeks. She had also skipped the last committee meeting and so was unaware that a wealthy parent had come forward with a donation to cover the full costs of the playframe. Gloria was furious that no one had told her – but, on reflection, also wondered if she should have asked.

The approval of others may be necessary for all sorts of reasons, some of which may seem irritating and bureaucratic, but it is important that everyone involved pulls together in full knowledge and agreement. In any case, the approval of others will give you the confidence to put your ideas into action, and will share the burden if things don't work out.

But let's be positive. If you plan and prepare carefully everything should work for you. The following samples of a fundraising strategy, a promotional plan and a proposal/discussion document should help to get you started. Have fun!

Sample documents

FUN (Fathers United for Nurturing) is a voluntary organization set up to promote the role of fathers in the upbringing of their children. Operating in the south-west corner of Surrey, it gives support by organizing activities to which fathers can bring their children, giving them confidence and enjoyment in being active parents.

Currently our organization is energetically led, but is not as well known in the community as it could be, and has insufficient funds for the programme of activities currently planned.

In particular we need to:

1   Promote our activities to potential users and funders.

2   Raise £12,000 to cover the costs of activities planned for the next 12 months.

3   Secure £3,000 as a base for the following 12 months.

We have two committed volunteers, one with promotional experience and the other with some limited fundraising experience who will work from home to implement our promotional plan and fundraising strategy.

FUN promotional plan

Introduction

We recognize that we will not be able to fundraise effectively if we have not made ourselves and our objectives known to the local community from which we hope to secure funds. This promotional plan is, therefore, designed to dovetail with, and support, our fundraising strategy.

Aim

To promote the work of FUN, particularly, but not exclusively, to men within our local community, in order to encourage donation of funds and participation in our activities.

Objectives

1 To develop a good working relationship with the *Paterbury Advertiser* and the *Paterbury Chronicle*, our local newspapers.
2 To secure coverage of each of FUN's activities in these papers.
3 To develop knowledge of and interest in FUN's work through contact with local businesses and men's clubs.

Messages

The key messages for all promotional activity are:

1 that FUN is fun!
2 that FUN is a worthy local cause for support.

Methods

1 To set up lunchtime meetings with the editors of our local papers (plus any journalists or correspondents who have shown a particular interest in men's issues) in order to build rapport, explain our work and explore ways in which we could provide interesting stories for publication. Also to learn how best to meet the papers' deadlines and find out what sort of photos and stories appeal most to their readers. Initial meetings to be set up by March and followed by further meetings or telephone contact as appropriate. Invitations to all FUN events to be issued to the local press as a matter of course. Include local papers

on our mailing lists for distribution of our own leaflets etc.

2 To identify the newsworthy or photogenic elements of each of our activities to ensure coverage in the local papers. To issue news releases or photocalls to meet the local papers' deadlines, offering words or pictures that will appeal to their readers. The first event will be the FUN splash at the Lido when it opens in May. Secure a celebrity 'Dad' and child to take the first plunge on our behalf – by April.

3 To start our own quarterly newsletter called 'The Fun' to promote our events and raise awareness of our needs for funds. 'The Fun' will be mailed to all our existing supporters, plus the Human Resources or Personnel departments of all our local companies, plus our local football, rugby, golf, Conservative and Working Mens Clubs. First issue to be published in June.

4 To secure presentations of our work to the local Chamber of Commerce and local branches of the Rotary and Lions clubs. Presentation dates to be confirmed by August and to take place through the autumn.

Timetable

February/March	Set up meetings with journalists
April	Secure celebrity for splash day
	Set up press coverage of splash day
	Start production work on 'The Fun'
May	Run splash day event
June	Publication of the first issue of 'The Fun'
July/August	Arrange presentations to Chamber of Commerce, Rotary and Lions
Ongoing	Following initial meetings – contact with journalists as appropriate
	As fundraising events are agreed – set up press coverage for each event.

Budget

We will need to spend the following:

Entertainment	£250
Newsletter production	£500 (£250 per issue – two issues this year)
Newsletter distribution	£500 (£250 per issue – two issues this year)
Presentation costs	£100
Phone/stationery	£300
Other expenses	£100
Total	£1,750

Review

The success of this plan will be reviewed by the trustees of FUN in November, following which and taking account of progress made, a plan will be drawn up for next year.

Approval

This plan was approved by the trustees of FUN in January.

FUN fundraising strategy

Introduction

Currently we have insufficient funds to cover our running expenses and the costs of all the events we have planned for this year. We have decided to introduce a small charge to fathers for participation in our activities, but do not want this to become prohibitive. We must, therefore, increase our fundraising efforts. We have put in place a promotional plan to raise our profile and will capitalize on this in our fundraising.

Aims

1 To raise £12,000 to cover this years' activities and expenses.
2 To raise a further £3,000 towards the cost of next year's activities and expenses.

Methods

1 To ask our local 4x4 car dealer, who is an active FUN supporter, to run a 4x4 'FUN day' that will promote his

vehicles and raise funds for FUN through a small entry fee, raffle and other fundraising stalls e.g. Aunt Sally (or Uncle Simon), coconut shy, strongest man etc. Agreement to be reached by March for the FUN day in June. Anticipated income after expenses deducted – £1,500. Extra volunteers will be needed to man the stalls.

2 To hold a major summer fundraising event – Jazz in the Park – in the grounds of Paterbury Manor, owned by our patron Sir Richard Mann. A committee will be recruited immediately to run this event. Sponsorship will be sought immediately from a local company to cover all the costs of the event so that ticket sales (500 tickets at £10 each) will be pure profit for FUN. Agreement to be reached in January for the event in July. Anticipated income £5,000.

3 To approach our local football, rugby, cycling, swimming and athletics clubs to run one sponsored event each on our behalf – FUN will play a coordinating role only. Agreement to be reached by April. Anticipated income £2,500.

4 To ask our local freehouse, the Prince of Wales, to donate 1p for every pint of beer sold throughout an agreed promotional period. Also to ask Prince of Wales customers to fill a magnum with coins. Agreement to be reached by March. Anticipated income £2,000.

5 To hold a sponsored FUN run for dads and kids in the grounds of Paterbury Manor in October. Agreement to be reached by May. All supporters (e.g. rugby club, football club, Prince of Wales etc.) to be mobilized! Anticipated income £3,000.

6 To find a sponsor to cover the costs of 'The FUN' newsletter. Agreement with sponsor to be reached by March. Anticipated income £1,000.

Many of our fundraising activities will offer opportunities to promote FUN. Likewise we will capitalize on the results of the promotional plan (e.g. contacts made through presentations to the Chamber of Commerce etc. to be approached for sponsorship). Fundraising and promotion will work hand-in-hand.

Timetable

January	Seek agreement for Jazz in the Park from all relevant parties
	Recruit committee to run event
	Seek sponsorship for Jazz in the Park
February	Seek agreement for 4x4 Fun Day
	Seek agreement for fundraising events at the Prince of Wales
	Seek sponsorship for 'The FUN' newsletter
	Agree terms of sponsorship for Jazz in the Park
March	Finalize plans for Jazz in the Park, 4x4 Fun Day, and Prince of Wales fundraising.
	Agree terms for sponsorship of 'The FUN'
April	Approach local clubs to run events on our behalf
	Seek agreement for FUN run
May	Finalize plans for FUN run
	Promote and organize 4x4 Fun Day and Jazz in the Park
	Finalize plans for FUN run
June	4x4 Fun Day
	Promote and organize Jazz in the Park
July	Jazz in the Park
	Promote and organize FUN run
September	Promote and organize FUN run
October	FUN run
November	Review
December	Well earned rest!

Budget

We will need to spend the following:

Expenses for running and promoting 4x4 FUN day	£100
Sponsorship approaches and materials for Jazz in the Park	£500
Sponsorship approaches for 'The FUN' newsletter	£100

FUN run sponsorship forms and promotional materials	£150
Phone/stationery etc.	£300
Other expenses	£100
Total	**£1,250**

NB   We believe that our ratio of expenses (£1,250) to income (£15,000) at less than 1:10 is acceptable and within accepted fundraising limits.

Review

The success of this plan will be reviewed in November. Lessons learned will be used to devise the plan for next year.

Approval

This fundraising strategy has been approved by the trustees of FUN.

FUN proposal/discussion document

To be accompanied by mission statement and other relevant materials.

Fitness and FUN

Proposal for a partnership between FUN and Paterbury Fitness Club

Introduction

FUN (Fathers United for Nurturing) believes that there are many ways in which it could work with the Paterbury Fitness Club for mutual benefit. Both organizations are keen to target men aged between 20 and 50 living in Paterbury. Both run activities to promote male fitness and fun. We would, therefore, like to propose an initial collaboration as set out in this document. We would like to emphasize that we are very open to Paterbury Fitness Club's own ideas and see this document as a starting point for discussion.

Sponsorship of FUN's new newsletter

FUN is soon to produce its first ever newsletter, aimed at raising awareness of FUN's activities and encouraging participation. It will be mailed to FUN's current list of supporters (around 100 fathers in the Paterbury area) as well as to all local sports clubs, businesses and other recreational organizations. Called 'The FUN', the newsletter will be quarterly, with two issues this year. FUN needs a sponsor to support this exciting new venture and believes that Paterbury Fitness Club would be the ideal partner.

Benefits to Paterbury Fitness Club as sponsor

1 Association with one of the most exciting and go-ahead voluntary groups in the area.
2 Perfect match of target customer profile – men aged 20 to 50 – and highly relevant link between fitness and fun.
3 Paterbury Fitness Club branding on front cover.
4 Paterbury Fitness Club feature in every issue.
5 Excellent joint PR opportunities – FUN may be able to secure celebrity endorsement of the project as well as local media coverage of the newsletter's launch.

Benefits to FUN

1 Costs of newsletter production covered.
2 Costs of mailing covered. We also hope that Paterbury Fitness Club would be happy to mail 'The FUN' to its own list of customers.
3 Partnership with an appropriate and well-respected local business.

Timeframe

We hope to reach a decision by the end of February so that the first issue of the newsletter can be mailed in June.

Costs

If current designs and mailing plans for 'The FUN' are agreed, the sponsorship will cost £1,000 in the first year and £2,000 for next year.

Conclusion

We believe that this project offers exciting opportunities for FUN and Paterbury Fitness Club to work together for mutual benefit. We would be delighted to discuss the sponsorship in greater detail and will call you next week to arrange a meeting.

And finally ...

Fundraising can be one of the greatest headaches or one of the most satisfying occupations, depending on how you approach it. If your mind-set is positive, you dedicate yourself to the task and you plan thoroughly before you start, you should get a tremendous buzz from your well-deserved success and from the relationships that you will build along the way. Fundraising is all about people – giving and taking, asking and receiving. There is pleasure to be gained from every aspect of the process. I hope that you will enjoy it.

Questions and answers

Having confidence

Q *I am quite good at planning. I work through everything logically and thoroughly so I know exactly what I need to do. The trouble is that I would rather plan something than actually go out and do it. I get awful nerves when I think about implementing my plan. What can I do?*

A In an ideal world you would probably be a strategic thinker. We all have strengths and weaknesses and you are lucky that you find planning easy. Others might envy those skills.

If you want to fundraise you have to 'make the ask' too. Try to take confidence from the fact that you are so well-prepared. Many others will not be. Use your strength to help you overcome your weakness.

Usually the first step into difficult territory is the worst. You will become more used to asking for money with practice. Experience in itself will give you confidence but focus too on the sense of satisfaction you will get when you achieve your goal. Allow the commitment you feel to your cause to drive you on, and anticipate the pleasure that will come with success.

Dovetailing organization and fundraising strategies

Q *I am frustrated because I have prepared a fundraising strategy for our small organization but my colleagues can't decide on a strategy for the organization as a whole. What can I do about this?*

A This is a difficult, but not uncommon, situation. It is essential that your organization does have a clear mission and strategy. Perhaps you could work with your colleagues to help them get their thoughts in order. If you are good at strategic planning, maybe you could draft a strategy for the organization for your colleagues to discuss and approve.

Once a sensible strategy is in place you should revisit your own fundraising plan to make sure that the two dovetail.

Finding a fundraising job

Q *I think fundraising is really exciting. I have done it on a voluntary basis. How can I go about making it my career?*

A Good for you! You will find plenty of fundraising jobs advertised in your local paper or the national press, particularly Monday's *Guardian*.

Or you could be more proactive and try targeting a few charities that appeal to you. Find out who handles recruitment and send your CV with a covering letter that will persuade them to meet you. Explain your voluntary fundraising experience and add details of any sales, marketing, or PR skills and qualifications that you may have. Computer literacy, administrative skills, and business, finance or project management experience could be relevant. You may have to wait for a vacancy to come up but at least you will be at the head of the queue and no one will doubt your motivation.

You may wish to undertake further training before you apply. Look in the Appendix for the names and contact details of organizations that offer courses. Some of the bigger charities can afford to offer training on the job. Good luck!

APPENDIX

Business in the Community
137 Shepherdess Walk
London N1 7RQ
Tel: 0870 600 2482
Email: information@bitc.org.uk
Website: www.bitc.org.uk
Organization for business people and companies supporting charities in a variety of ways.

Charities Aid Foundation
Kings Hill, West Malling
Kent ME19 4TA
Tel: 01732 520 000 Fax: 01732 520 001
Email: enquiries@caf.charitynet.org
Website: www.charitynet.org
CAF is a charity which helps donors make the most of their giving, and charities make the most of their resources. Makes grants and promotes tax-effective giving.

Charity Commission for England and Wales
London – Harmsworth House, 13–15 Bouverie Street
London EC4Y 8DP

Liverpool – 2nd Floor
20 Kings Parade
Queens Dock,
Liverpool L3 4DQ

Taunton – Woodfield House
Tangier
Taunton
Somerset TA1 4BL
Phone number for all offices: 0870 3330123
Website: www.charity-commission.gov.uk
Offers advice and information. Maintains Register of Charities.

Charity Commission Publications
Distribution Officer
Woodfield House
Tangier
Taunton
Somerset TA1 4BL
Answerphone order line: 01823 345427.
Website: www.charity-commission.gov.uk
Free publications covering all aspects of charities and the law.

Comic Relief
5th Floor
89 Albert Embankment
London SE1 7TP
Tel: 0207 820 5555 Fax: 0207 820 5500
Website: www.comicrelief.org.uk
Organizes Red Nose Day. Distributes grants to specific funding areas in the UK and Africa.

The Community Fund (previously the National Lottery Charities Board)
St Vincent House
16 Suffolk Street
London SW1Y 4NL
Tel: 0207 747 5300 Fax: 0207 747 5214
Website: www.community-fund.org.uk
Application forms: 0845 791 9191
Distributes money raised by the National Lottery.

Customs and Excise
All enquiries relating to VAT should be directed to your local Customs and Excise Office. Find the number in your phone directory.

Department of Health and Social Services
Voluntary Activity Unit
Charities Branch
Castle Buildings
Stormont
Belfast BT4 3RA
Tel: 02890 569314
The charity authority for Northern Ireland – offers advice.

Directory of Social Change
24 Stephenson Way
London NW1 2DP
Tel: 0207 209 5151   Fax: 0207 209 5049
Email: info@dsc.org.uk
Website: www.dsc.org.uk
Publishes a wide range of books and offers training on fundraising.

Fundraising UK Ltd
36 Palestine Grove
London SW19 2QN
Tel: 0208 640 5233
Website: www.fundraising.co.uk
Operates the useful UK Fundraising website.

FunderFinder
65 Raglan Road
Leeds LS2 9DZ
Tel: 0113 243 3008
Email: info@funderfinder.org.uk
Website: www.funderfinder.org.uk
Operates the FunderFinder software package.

Gaming Board of Great Britain
Lotteries Section
Berkshire House
169/173 High Holborn
London WC1V 7AA
Tel: 0207 306 6200
Website: www.gbgb.org.uk
Provides information about regulations concerning lotteries, especially where the sale of tickets will exceed £20,000.

Gifts in Kind UK
PO Box 140
4 St Dunstan's Hill
London EC3R 5HB
Tel: 0207 204 5003
Email: info@inkinddirect.org
Website: www.inkinddirect.org
Acts as a clearing house for businesses to donate surplus goods and equipment to the voluntary sector.

Institute of Charity Fundraising Managers (ICFM)
Market Towers
1 Nine Elms Lane
London SW8 5NQ
Tel: 0207 627 3436 Fax: 0207 627 3508
Email: enquiries@icfm.co.uk
Website: www.icfm.org.uk
Professional body for the fundraising industry. Holds lists of consultants.

IR Charities
Inland Revenue
St John's House
Merton Road
Bootle
Merseyside L69 9BB
Tel: 0151 472 6043
Website: www.inlandrevenue.gov.uk
Has a range of booklets about tax reliefs available to charities.

Lions Club International
267 Alcester Road South
Kings Heath
Birmingham B14 6BT
Tel: 0121 441 4544
Email: lionsmd105@lineone.net
Website: www.lions.org.uk

National Association of Councils of Voluntary Service (NACVS)
3rd Floor, Arundel Court
177Arundel Street
Sheffield S1 2NU
Tel: 0114 278 6636 Fax: 0114 278 7004
Email: nacvs@nacvs.org.uk
Website: www.nacvs.org.uk
Umbrella association for local Councils of Voluntary Service.

National Centre for Volunteering
Regents Wharf
8 All Saints Street
London N1 9RL
Tel: 0207 520 8900
Email: centrevol@aol.com
Website: www.volunteering.org.uk
Promotes excellence in volunteering by providing training, publications, events, conferences, and support networks.

National Council for Voluntary Organizations (NCVO)
Regents Wharf
8 All Saints Street
London N1 9RL
Tel: 0207 713 6161 Fax: 0207 713 6300
HelpDesk: 0800 729 8798
Email: ncvo@ncvo-vol.org.uk
Website: www.ncvo-vol.org.uk
Offers help and advice to all voluntary organizations.

National Lottery Charities Board – see the Community Fund

REACH
Bear Wharf
27 Bankside
London SE1 9ET
Tel: 0207 928 0452 Fax: 0207 928 0798
Email: volwork@btinternet.com
Website: www.volwork.org.uk
Offers a free service matching charities to volunteers with business or professional skills.

Rotary International Britain and Ireland
Kingwharton Road
Alcester
Warwickshire B49 6BP
Tel: 01789 765411
Email: secretary@ribi.org
Website: www.rotary-ribi.org
Offers humanitarian services to the community through local clubs of professional and business men and women. Try contacting your local club.

Scottish Charities Office
25 Chambers Street
Edinburgh EH1 1LA.
Tel: 0131 226 2626 Fax: 0131 226 6912
Website: www.crownoffice.gov.uk/charities
Supervises and regulates charities in Scotland.

Wales Council for Voluntary Action
Baltic House
Mount Stuart Square
Cardiff Bay
Cardiff CF10 5FH
Tel: 029 2043 1700
Email: enquiries@wcva.org.uk
Website: www.wcva.org.uk
Represents the interests of voluntary organizations in Wales,
providing information, consultancy, funding, management and
training services.

Working for a Charity
The Peel Centre
Percy Circus
London WC1X 9EY
Tel: 0207 833 8220
Email: enquiries@wfac.org.uk
Website: www.wfac.org.uk
Offers training to those wishing to move into the voluntary sector.

GLOSSARY

AIDA formula   A formula used by advertisers to focus on the key points of any advertisement – to grab **attention**, develop **interest**, create **desire**, and prompt **action**.

brainstorming   A method for generating ideas on a given subject. A group of people contributes in a process that is purely creative. No criticism is allowed and every idea must be recorded.

brand   The image or identity of a product or service, or even, loosely, of an organization.

case for support   A document that outlines why your cause or project is worthy of support.

core costs   The running costs of an organization or project – for example staff costs, rents and administration costs.

excepted charity   A charity which is allowed to register with the Charity Commission, but is not obliged to do so by law.

mail shot   A letter or leaflet that you mail to potential donors.

making the ask   The specific task of asking your donor for money, as opposed to that of explaining the need for funds or expanding on the merits of your cause.

marketing mix   The range of activities that make up the marketing process – getting the right product, at the right price, into the right place and promoting it well.

mission statement   A statement agreed by everyone in your organization that encapsulates the ethos of your organization and what you are trying to achieve.

PR   Public Relations, or the art of building good relationships with potential donors, supporters or other groups or individuals who might influence your activities.

press release   A brief document sent to the media to tell them about a newsworthy event or activity.

pyramid of giving   A model used by fundraisers to show the normal pattern of giving to a particular cause, project or appeal. It shows one or two major gifts at the top, supported by a broader layer of medium-sized donations, supported in turn by a broader layer of small donations at the base.

prospect   A potential donor or supporter. A warm prospect is one that you are likely to convert into a donor or supporter.

networking   Getting to know people and building useful relationships with them, often using one person to introduce you to another.

royalty   A percentage of the price of a product – often given to charities in exchange for endorsement of a commercial product.

SWOT   A model used to help identify **strengths**, **weaknesses**, **opportunities** and **threats**.

INDEX

ty TEACH YOURSELF

NEGOTIATING

Phil Baguley

Teach Yourself Negotiating is an important book for all professionals. The need to negotiate effectively exists at all levels in all organizations. Whether you are dealing with colleagues, suppliers or customers you need to be able to negotiate – and do it well.

A book you cannot afford to be without, *Teach Yourself Negotiating*:

- shows you how to prepare for, carry out and complete your negotiations
- helps you decide what strategies and tactics to use
- illustrates how to use the bargaining process to generate a successful outcome
- guides you to a successful implemention of that outcome
- provides a checklist for assessing your own negotiating skills.

Phil Baguley is an experienced business writer and lecturer. He has held senior management roles in multinational corporations and has also worked as a management consultant in the UK and Europe.

Other related titles

 TEACH YOURSELF

PUBLIC RELATIONS

Angela Murray

In the age of information and communication, public relations is now acknowledged as an essential part of any business that wants to succeed in a competitive world.

Teach Yourself Public Relations is a practical, no-nonsense guide which gives invaluable advice on implementing realistic and successful PR campaigns, including:

- Planning a PR campaign
- Gaining media coverage
- Direct communication
- Internal PR
- Crisis management

Angela Murray is a freelance PR consultant who has advised a wide range of businesses, from multi-nationals to small organizations.

TEACH YOURSELF

BUSINESS PRESENTATIONS

Angela Murray

Giving a presentation can be a daunting and nerve-racking experience, even for a regular presenter – what can you do to give yourself confidence and ensure success? *Teach Yourself Business Presentations* provides the answer. From defining the brief to post-presentation analysis, the book supplies a step-by-step guide to the skills and techniques needed to deliver an effective, engaging presentation.

Team presentations, presentations to colleagues, informative and persuasive presentations – appropriate techniques are considered for these and many more. Throughout the book imagination, innovation and creativity are all actively encouraged.

Covered in the book:

- strategic planning – defining and analysing a brief
- planning and research
- creativity
- communication skills
- audio-visual aids
- 'presentation etiquette' and personal presentation
- analysing performance.

An easy-to-read guide, full of hints and tips, this book provides support and guidance for the novice, and fresh ideas for the more experienced.

Angela Murray is a freelance Business Consultant in marketing communications and presentation skills.